Asperger Syndrome and the Elementary School Experience

Practical Solutions for Academic & Social Difficulties

Susan Thompson Moore, M.Ed.

Autism Asperger Publishing Company
P.O. Box 23173
Shawnee Mission, Kansas 66283-0173
www.asperger.net

© 2002 by Autism Asperger Publishing Co.
Reprinted 2006
P.O. Box 23173
Shawnee Mission, Kansas 66283-0173

Publisher's Cataloging-in-Publication
(provided by Quality Books, Inc.)

Moore, Susan Thompson.
    Asperger syndrome and the elementary school experience : practical solutions for academic & social difficulties. – 1st ed.
    p. cm.
    Includes bibliographical references and index.
    Library of Congress Control Number: 2002107394
    ISBN: 1-931282-13-7

    1. Autistic children–Education (Elementary)
    2. Asperger's syndrome. I. Title.

LC4717.5.M66 2002   371.94'72
                   QBI02-200491

This book is designed in Minion and Futura

Managing Editor: Kirsten McBride
Cover Design: Taku Hagiwara
Design and Production: Tappan Design

Printed in the United States of America

Dedicated To

Marilyn Anderson
Jason Backus
Sally Bligh
Bill Holaday
Jan Jakubiak
Sue Kelps
Barb Kirby
Debbie Mercer
Brenda Smith Myles
Gayle Napoli
Kathy Ruiz
Rose Marie Santelli
Kathy Schoengrund
Julie Trabaris
Pat Webster
Liane Holliday Willey
Donna Yule

Not only has your work provided my son with skills for success in school, but you have helped create a world in which he feels free to be himself. For this, I thank you.

– Susan Thompson Moore

Contents

CHAPTER ONE

What Is Asperger Syndrome?

The characteristics that are now known as Asperger Syndrome were first identified in 1944 by a pediatrician in Vienna, Austria, Dr. Hans Asperger. His findings remained unknown in many parts of the world because they were published in only one language – German. In the 1980s, however, Dr. Asperger's findings were translated into English, and in the early 1990s the international medical community began to recognize and accept Asperger Syndrome (AS) as one of the exceptionalities within the autism spectrum that results in myriad challenges, including social and communication problems.

AS is a neurobiological disorder that is the result of any number of causes, including genetics, brain insult, or brain disease (Frith, 1991). It is listed as one of the pervasive developmental disorders along with autism, Rett's Disorder, childhood disintegrative disorder, and pervasive developmental disorder-not otherwise specified (American Psychiatric Association, 2000) in the *Diagnostic and Statistical Manual of Mental Disorders – Text Revision 2000*, one of the resources used by medical professionals for diagnosing Asperger Syndrome. Like other pervasive developmental disorders, Asperger

Syndrome falls on a continuum, with behavioral manifestations and communication impairments ranging from mild to severe. Most sets of criteria used to diagnose AS include impairments in social interaction, communication, and flexible thinking. However, some individuals with AS also experience difficulties with sensory integration, language development, and motor functioning. Making diagnosis even more difficult, some students with AS exhibit few, if any, autistic traits and behaviors unless they are under stress. Others display stereotyped behaviors, anxiety, withdrawal, social difficulties, and communication problems on a daily basis.

As a pervasive disorder, AS affects an individual in many ways. Even though it can be defined by a set of criteria, it is important to note that AS affects individuals differently. In making the diagnosis, a diagnostician will need assessments of behavior, interactions, and cognitive functioning from school and home. In addition, the diagnosis should be made and confirmed by professionals familiar with the disorder and the various ways in which it is manifested.

This book provides educators with an understanding of AS and how it affects a student academically and socially, and provides specific strategies for helping elementary school students with AS function successfully. Chapter Two presents the major areas of difficulty for individuals with AS with examples of each so readers may develop an understanding of their students' diagnosis and its impact within the school setting. Typically, students with AS display difficulties in pragmatic language, social interactions, sensory processing, motor functioning, and cognition. After this general introduction, a series of chapters focus on specific interventions. For example, in Chapter Three, organizational accommodations are presented, while Chapter Four consists of recommendations for modifying curriculum. In Chapter Five, the focus shifts to the social problems of children with AS and provides step-by-step procedures for developing and enhancing social skills. Finally, because many individuals are involved in meeting the needs of students with AS, the importance of a team approach is emphasized in Chapter Six.

Throughout this book, you will find forms, organizational tools, and visuals that have been designed to help teachers and parents implement the recommended strategies. Personal accounts from my experience as a parent of a child with AS and as a teacher in the elementary grades are also included. To further illustrate, I have included personal experiences from other children with AS and from other teachers and therapists who work with students with AS. Through the use of personal accounts and firsthand experiences as a parent and teacher, my intention has been to emphasize the importance of viewing and treating students with AS with respect and understanding them as individuals with a neurobiological disorder who possess great potential for success in life.

. . . Understanding them as individuals with a neurobiological disorder who possess great potential for success in life.

CHAPTER TWO

The Five Areas of Impairment

This chapter provides an overview of the challenges and gifts that accompany Asperger Syndrome (AS) based on both my personal experience as a mother of a son with AS and my professional experience as a teacher. The chapter is divided into five sections: language development, social interaction, sensory integration, motor functioning, and cognitive processing. A child diagnosed with AS may or may not exhibit all of the behaviors and impairments discussed in this chapter, or she may exhibit them to different degrees. However, any combination of these behaviors and impairments will affect a person's ability to relate to peers, communicate effectively with others, and perform well at school. The extent to which these problems affect the student in the school setting is individual as well as situational.

It is important to become familiar with the typical behaviors and impairments associated with AS and the impact they have on a student diagnosed with this disorder.

Language Development

Language development may be affected by AS on multiple levels: phonemic, semantic, syntactic, and pragmatic. At first, most people do not recognize the language peculiarities of children with AS as problematic because they often sound like effective communicators. That is, many students with AS have large vocabularies, pronounce multisyllabic words with ease, and use these words in a seemingly appropriate manner. However, as shown below, many have language problems nevertheless (see Table 2.1).

TABLE 2.1
Language-Related Characteristics of Children with AS

- Odd speech that may be pedantic in quality, repetitive, and/or perseverative
- Unnatural rhythm or rate of speech
- Monotone or unnatural inflection
- Inappropriate speech volume
- Idiosyncratic use of words
- Excessive, minimal, or selective talking that is inappropriate for a given situation or age of child
- Literal interpretation of language
- Inability to comprehend tone, inflection, and/or word emphasis
- Inability to interpret nonverbal language
- Reduced ability to communicate and/or comprehend verbal language when anxiety is high

---

Phonemic *(The Sounds of Letters)*

Some children with AS enunciate every letter and syllable in a precise, exaggerated, and pedantic manner. These children may even over-enunciate, changing words such as *ladder* to *latter* because they think that the middle sound in the word should be pronounced *t* like in the word *butter*. Similarly, they may say *mittle* for *middle* and *wintow* for *window.* In other words, they fail to recognize differences and variability within the sounds of the language and follow language rules to the extreme. Showing them the spelling of the words and rehearsal with a speech-language pathologist will help remediate this problem. It is also a good idea to try to coordinate this effort with the child's parents so they can reinforce the correct pronunciations outside of school.

Semantic *(The Meaning of Words)*

Often the speech of children with AS is impressive to adults. In fact, many sound like little "professors," using sophisticated vocabulary and phrasing. When James, a third-grade student with AS, was asked if he knew if the Quetzalcoatlus was a big dinosaur, he replied, "Actually, the Quetzalcoatlus was not a dinosaur. It was a winged reptile, meaning it's part of the Pteradactylan family. The Quetzalcoatlus had a 40 ft. wingspan." Like James, many children with AS have an incredible rote memory and are more than likely repeating words or lines they have memorized from books, videos, television, video games, and so on. Don't be fooled. Often, students with AS use pat responses they have memorized as a means to communicate. You cannot assume they understand every word or phrase they say.

During a poetry assignment, a second-grader with AS used the word *noble* to describe his parents. His teacher was so impressed with his vocabulary that she sent a note home to the boy's parents sharing her excitement. When the boy's mother asked her son if he knew the definition of the word *noble,* he responded, "It means *familiar.*" He then told his mother that he liked the way the word sounded and had used it for that reason.

Here is where the confusion lies: Children with AS do not know the meaning of some of the words they use, often using words based on criteria other than semantics alone. For example, a boy with AS used lines from Winnie the Pooh videos in his writing assignments exactly as they appeared in the videos. He wrote, "The boy was so happy. He was bouncy, trouncy, flouncy, pouncy. He had fun, fun, fun!" His teacher recognized the lines from the cartoons because shortly after she began teaching this student, she started watching Winnie the Pooh videos with her own 2-year-old son.

Many children with AS use a line they have heard in a movie or television show as a way to engage a peer in a conversation or to get attention because they have not learned how to use words to convey intentions. Colin, an 8-year-old with AS, would walk up to other children and begin reciting facts about the sinking of the Titanic he had heard while watching a documentary. The other children would just stare and walk away. His intention was to interact with them, but the message he sent was not clear to those around him.

Some children with Asperger Syndrome invent their own words and phrases that are not real words such as *oohaddy*, which meant *nice* to one young girl. Others create unique phrases such as *yesterday's night* to mean last night, developmentally appropriate for a 5-year-old but not a 9-year-old. Not surprisingly, these semantic problems make it difficult for children with AS to communicate effectively with peers and teachers. To help remedy this situation, check their understanding of words and phrases they use in their spoken or written language. Become familiar with their favorite interest, books, and videos to identify words and phrases that they are using incorrectly, and provide the support they need to work on their communication skills.

Children with autism begin to acquire language solely as a function of needs, as opposed to learning language as a means to interact with others (Koegel & Koegel, 1995) as in typical language development. Language development in children with AS often begins the same way. That is, they use language to make requests to satisfy their own needs, not to interact. By not using language as a social act, they do not acquire the communicative competence that their neurotypical peers learn in social interactions. Furthermore, they have difficulty using words spontaneously and combining them appropriately (Michael Thompson Productions & Bligh, 2000).

For example, when my son was 5 years old, he did not know how to ask for help. Neurotypical children learn from experience that they can obtain help with a task by forming a question such as, "Will you help me find the missing piece in this puzzle?" My son was not able to do this because he lacked the ability to formulate a question spontaneously, and he lacked the ability to acquire language skills while interacting with other children. While other children were learning how to formulate a question to get their needs met, my son played alone or near other children, but was unaware of how they communicated with each other.

When very young, children with AS often do not recognize their own feelings of hunger, exhaustion, or over-stimulation. Similarly, by school age, they do not recognize their own anxiety and feelings of distress or anger. They tend to react to such feelings by screaming, tantruming, or shutting down rather than using words to communicate their feelings or wants. Often those around the child learn to connect the inappropriate behaviors with specific needs the child may have, thereby further impeding language acquisition. In other words, teachers and parents begin to react to the child's behaviors in a way that reinforces them rather than encouraging proper language usage or development.

For example, Lara learned that she could get a drink by sitting on the floor and humming. Mike realized that he could get the teacher to exclude him from something he did not want to do if he stood up and started to whine and cry. This is not to say that these children are not communicating or should be punished for inappropriate behavior. Rather, they should be encouraged to use words and/or appropriate signs or symbols to convey messages, and all attempts to do so should be positively reinforced.

As children with AS get older, they pick up phrases from unnatural situations like a movie or from natural situations that are not related to the present situation and use those phrases as a means of meeting their needs. For example, Paul wanted permission to play a video game. He approached his mother and asked if she wanted help cleaning the house. She told him that she did not need his help but appreciated his offer anyway. Hearing this, Paul proceeded to drop to the floor and begin to cry. His mother did not understand why her son was so upset. Going over the situation in her mind, she suddenly remembered that a few days earlier she had rewarded Paul for helping with the household chores by allowing him extra time to play his video game. As he lay there on the floor crying, she calmly asked him if he wanted to play a video game. He stopped crying immediately and nodded. He was allowed to play. Later in the day, Paul's mother discussed the miscommunication with her son, explaining that if he wanted to play a video game, he was to say, "May I play a video game?" rather than ask to help clean the house.

With instruction, practice, and rehearsal, children with AS can learn to use language appropriately. What they say is not always what they are trying to communicate. The best approach to dealing with situations like this is to maintain patience and a calm demeanor (Myles & Southwick, 1999). Had Paul's mother in the above example not tried to interpret her son's message, his meltdown may have escalated.

> *With instruction, practice, and rehearsal, children with AS can learn to use language appropriately.*

Syntax (Grammar)

In addition to semantic problems, many children with AS also have difficulty with grammar. For example, they may use incorrect word order, causing confusion for others. Heather, a 7-year-old, referred to her dog as "that dog adorable is mine," reversing the standard English word order of adjective and noun.

Correct usage of prepositions can also be problematic. Individuals with AS may have trouble appropriately using the prepositions *to, for, in, on, of, with, at,* and *from* because prepositions are somewhat abstract and some rely on perspective-taking – difficult concepts for people with AS. For instance, Colin has difficulty with the prepositions *in* and *on.* He says that he is standing *in* the sidewalk rather than *on* the sidewalk and that his present is *for* John rather than *from* John. It may be helpful to provide individual instruction when you notice these errors and consult with the speech-language pathologist to assist you.

Some people with AS are so caught up in the language rules that they cannot listen to spoken language for its content because they are constantly checking for preciseness, noting every mispronunciation and grammatical error they think they hear. Some verbalize the corrections to the speaker as he is speaking, impeding the communication process as well as possibly offending the speaker. Practice and rehearsal with an adult is the best way to teach the student how to attend to the meaning of the message rather than its grammatical structure. A good approach is the activity called *Think It, Don't Say It* from the *Friends for Me* social skills program (Moore, 2002). This activity helps the student learn to keep some thoughts to herself through identification of inappropriate statements, modeling, and rehearsal.

Another way to help the student focus on meaning rather than grammar is to use a reward system for refraining from interrupting and correcting grammar during a role-play situation. Begin by discussing a favorite topic with the student while you keep control of the conversation and do most of the talking. As the student becomes engaged in the topic, start committing grammar errors and reward the student every few minutes while you are talking. Do not stop the conversation to reward. Just mark points or give stickers and other incentives as you keep talking. Likewise, reward the student if she responds to a question or statement appropriately, sticks to the topic, and/or ignores grammatical errors. As the student becomes proficient at maintaining a conversation about a favorite topic without interrupting and pointing out grammar errors, switch to topics that are unfamiliar to her. Now she will have to focus much more intently to keep from pointing out the grammar errors because she may not be as interested in the topic and, therefore, will be more likely to listen to the speaker's grammar and word choice rather than the content.

In another approach the roles are reversed so the student with AS becomes the one who is interrupted. Ask her to talk about a topic she really likes and interrupt her frequently to question her grammar and to correct her. This will help show her how difficult it is to maintain the topic when one is constantly being interrupted. It serves a dual purpose: The student gets practice in ignoring extraneous information *and* learns about perspective-taking.

Another common syntax problem among individuals with AS is their tendency to use language very formally. This often makes them the subject of ridicule because they do not speak like their classmates. Paul prefers to use *with whom* and *for whom* in his everyday speech, which is not common among neurotypical children. For example, he says, "That is the boy with whom I went to the library." While grammatically correct, this statement is much more formal in structure than that used by his peers. Identifying such phrases as being used for *writing* rather than *conversation* will help children with AS learn how to use formal and informal speech appropriately for specific social situations. Because they think in black and white terms, it is easy for them to learn phrases that fit into categories. For example, they may be taught phrases to be used for writing, those to be used when talking with friends, and those to be used when talking with adults.

As mentioned earlier, children with AS generally do not learn language from social situations, including picking up the grammar of other children. In order to facilitate language learning for the child with AS, it is helpful to have the child watch a video of neurotypical children interacting to help point out the way they speak. Basically, it is similar to teaching a foreign language to someone who has a good vocabulary, but does not know all of the grammar rules and thus sounds odd when tying to speak.

Pragmatics *(The Communicative Intent of Language)*

Pragmatics is the area of language where children with AS experience the greatest problems. At this level, a speaker conveys meaning through such techniques as vocal inflection, volume, body language, and hidden curriculum (Myles & Southwick, 1999). Individuals with AS are often blind and deaf to these means of communicating, and therefore are at a great disadvantage when meaning must be obtained from tone of voice, use of idioms, use of sarcasm, and nonverbal gestures. For example, the student with AS may be confused by or misinterpret a statement like the following:

Do you want to do that?

There are several ways to interpret that statement, depending upon where the emphasis and inflection is placed. For example, when the speaker places the emphasis on the word *you*, the question has an entirely different intended meaning than if the emphasis is placed on the word *that*. Likewise, the meaning will change if the emphasis is placed on the word *want*. The following examples demonstrate this point.

Question: Do *you* want to do that?

Implied meaning: Do you, as opposed to another person, want to do that?

Question: Do you want to do *that?*

Implied meaning: Do you want to do that, rather than something else.

Question: Do you *want* to do that?

Implied meaning: Do you want to do that, or is someone making you do that?

The questions contain the same words, said in the same order. However, each question implies something different because the placement of word emphasis is different.

The speaker's tone and volume also affect the meaning implied in a statement. We use variations in word emphasis, inflection, tone, and volume to add information or implied meaning to a statement or question. However, children with AS often miss these subtleties, unable to determine implied meaning. When teaching these children, therefore, it is best to check frequently for understanding, avoid sarcasm, and provide directions in simple terms, backed by written instructions.

Vague terminology

In addition to difficulty interpreting the pragmatic features of language, children with AS also have problems understanding vague terminology as well as interpreting idioms, certain phrases, and some expressions that are commonly used by their peers and teachers.

Individuals with AS think in black and white, right or wrong, rule-imposed terms.

Individuals with AS think in black and white, right or wrong, rule-imposed terms. Therefore, unspecific terminology evokes confusion and anxiety. It is best to avoid words and phrases such as *later, in a few minutes, maybe,* and so on. Point out precisely how many minutes until reading group starts and if they will or will not have homework tonight. Vagueness may start children with AS on a repetitive sequence of question asking or monologuing, or possibly even meltdowns. Remember, they are not doing this to annoy anyone. They are simply trying to make sense of their world and have a very difficult time when they cannot comprehend what we say.

Literal interpretation

Another language problem experienced by students with AS is that they tend to interpret language literally, sometimes leading to anger or confusion. At dinner one night, Jamie read the writing on the box of the takeout pizza his dad had brought home. When finished reading, Jamie asked his father to call the restaurant where he had bought the pizza. Jamie's father questioned his son *WHY*, to which Jamie responded that the writing on the box said to "call right away if not 100% satisfied with your order." Probing further, the father asked if he liked the pizza. Jamie answered, "Yes, but I am not *completely* satisfied. It could be a bit better. Therefore, I am NOT 100% satisfied so we MUST call the restaurant!" When his father tried to explain that they should call only if the pizza were burned or inedible for some reason, Jamie commented, "Well, why don't they just write *THAT* on the box?"

Another example of literal interpretation happened with a teacher and Louis, her 9-year-old student with AS, on a class field trip. As they were about to cross the street, the teacher told the class, "Keep your heads up while crossing the street." Louis certainly did – in fact, he kept his head up so well that he was able to tell the other children about an airplane he saw overhead. The teacher chuckled and explained to the boy that "heads up" in this case meant to be aware of oncoming traffic and to look both ways before crossing. Not surprisingly, Louis commented, "If that's what you want us to do, why do you tell us to put our heads up?"

A little humor and a great deal of patience will go a long way. Students with AS can be trying at times, but they sure can make your day interesting! They keep you on your toes. (Try explaining that one to your student with AS!)

The previous examples illustrate problems that children with AS have in interpreting language. The communication process is further complicated for these children because they also have difficulty conveying their own messages due to the language problems inherent to AS. That is, their expressive language is poor because:

- They use words and sentences oddly, as seen in the above examples.
- They fail to use body language or use it inappropriately.
- They talk too much or too little.
- The quality of their voice is unusual.

Lack of or inappropriate use of body language

Children with AS often do not use body language as a means to communicate. For example, when my son is trying to communicate that he has not understood something, he does not make eye contact with the speaker, move in closer, turn his head to the side, furl his eyebrows, or raise his hand like neurotypical children may do. Instead, he has a stoic look on his face, remains silent, and does nothing with his body to communicate that he has not understood what was said to him. The only way the speaker may discover that he has not understood is to ask him directly if he has understood what was said.

Other children with AS demonstrate body language that is misunderstood by others. For example, Kelvin stands too far from people and with his arms folded, giving the impression that he is not interested in what others have to say. But in reality, Kelvin is very interested in interacting with the other children, he just does not know how to use body language to display interest. Another boy with AS does not show any emotion in his face. His paraprofessionals and teachers have to interpret his behavior for the other children in the room so they know when he is feeling angry, sad, or confused.

Excessive, perseverative talking

Many children with AS talk excessively – perseverating on a topic, monopolizing a conversation, or engaging in repetitive speech patterns or questioning. They are not doing this to annoy. Due to their inability to understand social cues, read body language, and recognize facial expressions, they do not know when to shift topics or when to stop talking. At times, especially when their anxiety level is high, they have difficulty shifting focus or answering others' questions. This elevated level of anxiety may also result in repetitive and perseverative language. In such instances, social skills and language/communication training with a speech-language pathologist is necessary, as well as assistance from the classroom teacher. A social skills training program called Social Language Groups (Michael Thompson Productions & Bligh, 2000) has proven very successful for teaching children with AS how to engage in reciprocal communication and interpret pragmatic language. This program also helps reduce or eliminate the tendencies to monologue, repeat phrases or questions, and interrupt (see Chapter Five for a discussion of Social Language Groups).

> *. . . They can be taught specific rules for communication.*

Because students with AS tend to be rule-driven, they can be taught specific rules for communication. For example, children who talk on and on about their favorite subject, ignoring cues from listeners who are losing interest, need a communication rule to teach them how to communicate effectively. Sally Bligh, a speech-language pathologist recognized worldwide for her work with children with AS and autism, suggests giving the student with AS a rule such as the following:

Say two things and then ask a question.

This rule is easily understood by the child, but she will need assistance in remembering to follow it when she has begun perseverating, monologuing, or engaging in repetitive speech patterns.

Rick, a fifth-grader, is fascinated by elevators and has a vast knowledge about the history of elevators. When trying to communicate with his peers, he generally monologues about elevators, providing name after name of elevators he has ridden on or read about, giving specific information about the manufacturer, the year a given elevator was put into use, its serial number, and other facts. In order to help Rick learn to end his monologuing style of speaking, the speech-language pathologist frequently reminded him of the rule: *Say two things and then ask a question,* before it was his turn to speak. As Rick began to monologue, the speech-language pathologist interrupted him, reminded him of the rule again, and then prompted him with a question if he was unable to generate one on his own.

This strategy can be used not only in a therapeutic setting but also during natural settings such as when the student with AS is involved in group activities or interacting with peers during recess. Be sure that all adults involved in teaching and/or providing assistance to students with AS become familiar with the perseverative/excessive talking that many children with AS engage in and methods for assisting them in controlling it.

Minimal talking

Some children with AS speak minimally, speak only selectively, or are sometimes considered "selectively mute." This behavior may be a response to anxiety or a sensory issue. Therefore, forcing or coercing the child to speak only worsens the problem. Instead, use specific techniques to help the child become familiar and comfortable with her environment. One way to help the child speak to others, as well as improve social skills and develop a friendship with a peer, is to use the social skills activities and Social Language Groups discussed in Chapter Five. As the child becomes less anxious, develops some social skills, and becomes familiar with classmates, his expressive language will increase. For children who have great difficulty speaking due to anxiety, request the help of a social worker or school psychologist who is skilled in working with children with AS. For children who are reluctant to speak because of sensory problems, identify the sensory issues with the help of an occupational therapist and family members, try to reduce or eliminate the environmental factors that are disturbing to the child, and encourage and reward the child for speaking.

Quality of speech

The quality of speech may also be affected; this is known as dysprosody. The speech of individuals with AS may be characterized by an unnatural tone and rhythm, odd inflections, or inappropriate volume. Some children with AS have a singsong quality to their speech while others sound monotone. Furthermore, the rate of speech may be extreme – either very rapid or deliberately slow.

Arlen, an 8-year old with AS, speaks very slowly, elongating vowels and extending the length of words. Neurotypical children have difficulty understanding his speech and avoid engaging in conversations with him for that reason. My son's speech can be quite rapid, causing his listeners confusion. Even when a listener asks him to repeat what he just said, he often merely repeats the statement equally as fast as the first time. A 7-year-old girl with AS speaks so quietly that other children choose not to play with her. They cannot hear anything she says so they interpret that as disinterest and bypass her as a choice for a playmate. Another example of expressive language problems is seen in the speech of Miguel, an 11-year-old with AS. Miguel raises the pitch of the last word in every sentence he says. This makes his speech sound very odd to neurotypical children, yet Miguel is completely unaware that he is doing it.

In creating and implementing a plan for therapy and remediation of dysprosody, it is important that all teachers, staff members, and family members work together. Ask the speech-language pathologist to meet with the school team and the child's parents to explain the problems. Once the problems are identified, the speech-language pathologist may suggest intervention, practice, and reinforcement techniques for the team and family to use. Furthermore, if a child needs therapy, it must be provided.

It is important that all teachers, staff members, and family members work together.

In addition to the therapy provided by a speech-language pathologist, the classroom teacher and support staff may have to address the dysprosody problem. To do so, make an audio recording of the child's speech. Select a couple of sections and transcribe it. Next, record neurotypical children repeating the same lines using natural inflection, rate, volume, and so on. Now have the student with AS try to mimic the speech pattern of the neurotypical child. It is also helpful to record the student with AS to show her the progress she is making in changing her speech patterns. It will take individual instruction, coaching, and repeated practice, sometimes for weeks and months, as well as coaching in natural contexts for the student to change her prosody. However, it can be done. Consistency and regular practice yield the greatest results.

Speaking style

As discussed in the syntax section of this chapter, children with AS have difficulty adjusting their speaking style to fit a given situation. Robert, a teen with AS, spoke to classmates as if he were in front of a group of scientists at a chemistry symposium. Using scientific terminology, he spoke in a very precise and pedantic manner, clearly enunciating every word in a stiff and unnatural style. Robert's classmates did not understand that he had a language problem. They simply viewed him as odd and chose to ignore him. Using a completely different vocabulary and inflection than Robert, his neurotypical peers usually say, "Hey! How's it going?" to greet each other. In response, they say, "It's going OK. How about you?" By comparison, Robert's typical greeting to his peers is, "Hello. Last night on the Discovery Channel I saw a program on genetic engineering in cancer research," said in a robot-like, monotone voice with little or no inflection, no eye contact, and no pause for a response. Robert's speaking style may be appropriate for a classroom lecture, but it is not appropriate for engaging in reciprocal peer interactions.

Teach students with AS how to use a variety of speaking styles and how to monitor and regulate their speech. Keep in mind when teaching these concepts that accepting change does not come easily to individuals with AS. They will more than likely try to convince you that other people should speak like they do. Do not engage in a verbal battle. Instead, take time to raise their awareness of the various styles and manners of speaking.

Students with AS generally need to be taught language differences individually. Record conversations of neurotypical children interacting. At first, use an audio tape to focus on the words and inflection. Transcribe the dialogue for the student with AS and have her read the lines as if they were lines in a play. Repeated practice will help lock her peers' phrasing and vocabulary in her memory. Coach the student as she "learns" her lines. As she starts to use the lines and inflections correctly, introduce appropriate body language and practice by role-playing specific situations like greetings, asking for help with schoolwork, or inviting someone to play. When proficient at this level, allow the student time to practice with a cooperative peer. Follow this by coaching in natural situations until the student is able to adjust her speech appropriately to specific situations.

Most children with AS experience expressive and receptive language problems while acquiring language. These problems often persist into adolescence and early adulthood, making students seem younger than they actually are. For example, errors that are typical of a 4-year-old may be found in an 11-year-old student with AS. Young children frequently repeat the question word "why" over and over when they are engaging in a conversation with an adult. While it can be tiring to the adult, it is expected and accepted that young children ask the same question repeatedly. When an 11-year-old does the same thing, however, it is no longer expected and accepted. Similarly, a 4-year-old may not understand idioms such as "it is raining cats and dogs" and run to the window to look for the falling cats and dogs – an expected behavior in a 4-year-old. However, when the 11-year-old student with AS fails to understand the idiom and runs to the window, it is usually perceived as immature behavior.

> **Most children with AS experience expressive and receptive language problems.**

When working with a student with AS, keep in mind that his ability to "mimic" language is often good, but his ability to comprehend language is not. Sometimes it is difficult to understand that children who have such incredibly rich and extensive vocabularies really do have language problems.

The language-related problems of students with AS are often subtle and difficult to identify unless you carefully analyze their expressive and receptive language competency in natural settings. That is, teachers and therapists must take into consideration the student's actual mastery of the language as opposed to her superficial display of proficiency. To that end, the student's language must be evaluated through observations in many different settings and by several different specialists, including the speech-language pathologist, teacher, social worker, and psychologist. Careful and specific analysis of the student's language will enable teachers and therapists to provide the appropriate language instruction and accommodations needed to help the student work up to his potential and develop communication skills for life beyond school.

Social Interaction

Children with AS often lack a social sense and demonstrate limited, but intense emotions. This, coupled with their language impairments, adversely affects their success in social interactions and may lead to withdrawal, aggression, depression, and/or anxiety. As a result, they need constant coaching and facilitation during *all* types of social interactions from small-group activities to the lunch/recess break until they have gained some proficiency at interacting and have developed confidence in their ability to interact with others. For some children, this may take a month or two. For others, it may not happen. Regardless, a support system must be in place for the entire school year.

A list of the major social characteristics of children with AS is found in Table 2.2. Four areas of concern in understanding and addressing the social problems of students with AS are: engaging in a conversation, social code of conduct, emotions, and dealing with change.

Engaging in a Conversation

As a result of their social and language deficits, children with AS have difficulty initiating and maintaining a conversation. That is, they do not know how to begin a conversation and engage a listener, nor do they know how to be a good listener. Further, their eye contact may be minimal, intense, or unnatural, giving the impression of disinterest or disagreement. The more they concentrate on what is being said, the more they look away from the speaker's face because it is often easier for individuals with AS to understand information

TABLE 2.2
Social Characteristics of Children with AS

- Lack of skills to establish friendships
- Difficulty initiating and/or maintaining conversations
- Difficulty discerning appropriateness of topic
- Personal-space violations
- Minimal, intense, or unnatural eye contact
- Inappropriate affective expression or response
- Lack of appropriate body language
- Inability to read body language and facial expressions
- Passivity
- Aggressiveness
- Inappropriate turn-taking
- Lack of awareness or disinterest in popular fads and trends
- Lack of interest in making friends
- Difficulty with perspective-taking (i.e., "theory of mind" deficits)

when they do not have to process auditory and visual information simultaneously. Unfortunately, others may perceive this behavior as aloofness or indifference.

Children with AS have difficulty with perspective-taking, also known as "theory of mind" deficits. That is, when speaking to others, they fail to take into consideration what their listeners may be thinking. Consequently, as mentioned before, they often take control of a conversation, speaking only about topics of interest to them and therefore often annoying their peers. When their ability to reciprocate interactions is limited, these children frequently find themselves outside the social circles, leading to feelings of isolation and ostracism.

William, a 6-year-old with AS, talks about Pokémon™ all the time. He typically begins talking about Pokémon characters or new strategies he has learned while playing a Pokémon video game as soon as he approaches another person. This frustrates the neurotypical children who have tired of listening to details about Pokémon, but William fails to change the topic because he cannot take others' perspective. He has no understanding of social cues and body language and does not know that he is annoying the other children. As a result, he has difficulty establishing and maintaining friendships.

Phil, a 12-year-old with AS, described the pain he felt when he was ignored by his peers. As he recounted his story, tears rolled down his cheeks. He was very troubled by the situation. Phil knew that he was not liked by the other students. He wanted to be accepted and liked, but lacked the skills to do so. Like Phil, many children with AS truly want friends. They just lack the skills to find them and to maintain the friendship.

When at the playground, my son would run in circles around the other children. He would remain at the periphery, hoping that the other children would come over and play with him. He lacked the ability to begin a conversation or the knowledge to join the others in their games. When children did approach him, he would begin reciting lines from Godzilla movies and roaring like Godzilla. The other children were not familiar with Godzilla movies and did not enjoy listening to movie lines or facts about Godzilla. Even though my son wanted to play, he did not how to engage in a conversation to let others know.

Social Code of Conduct

Children with AS also lack knowledge of the social codes of conduct such as turn-taking, respect for personal space, and appropriateness of topic. And because they lack the skills necessary to establish friendships, they may appear passive or aggressive, turning away potential friends.

Students with AS often lack interest in popular fads or trends, further alienating them from their peers. Furthermore, not knowing how to engage in a conversation, they may engage in repetitive psychomotor behaviors such as hand-flapping, spinning, or vocalizations that neurotypical children find strange or humorous. By learning social rules and developing social language skills (see Chapter Five), they can develop an awareness of what their peers typically talk about, what they like to play, and how they play, enabling them to find success in interactions and eliminating the inappropriate behaviors such as hand-flapping and spinning.

Students with AS need guidance, support, and coaching to compensate for their lack of social skills. It is simple to help foster a friendship. For example, the teacher can invite the student with AS and one of his classmates to have lunch with her, or allow them to go to the library or do a computer program together.

To learn to understand social codes of contact, students with AS require an interpreter (Myles & Adreon, 2001). Think of them as you would international students who do not speak your language. Many of the things you would do to accommodate an exchange student or a student whose first language is not English would work for students with AS. For example, they need specific, direct instruction in determining appropriate interpersonal space. Further, they require explanations of others' nonverbal communications such as folded arms or hands on hips, and translation of common phrases used by their peers such as "that rocks," which is used by my son's peers to mean that they really like something. As you interpret others' behaviors, gestures, and words for them, children with AS will gain the tools they need to help themselves navigate through the complexities of the social world.

Students with AS require an interpreter.

Emotions

Individuals with AS are not without feelings, but the manner in which they display them is often quite different from the way others do. For example, children with AS may exhibit little affect or emotional response unless they are anxious or frightened. Some simply shut down and withdraw, whereas others react more severely, displaying anxiety, fear, or anger with great fortitude! An otherwise passive, compliant child may erupt like a volcano in less than 30 seconds if feeling threatened, confused, overwhelmed, or overstimulated. She may cry, scream, panic, tantrum, withdraw, or engage in destructive or self-injurious behavior.

Individuals with AS are not without feelings.

Lakeesha, a first-grader with AS, pulls her hair out or says she wants to kill herself when she becomes upset. This extreme reaction may be prompted by something otherwise minor, such as becoming confused by an adult's behavior or words. For example, Lakeesha has pulled her hair out when she was told to end an activity. She had prior knowledge that the activity would last for 20 minutes and knew the time period was about to end, but she misinterpreted the teacher's remarks about ending the activity. She viewed it as a punishment rather than simply the end of an activity. Whereas most neurotypical children would ask the teacher if they were "in trouble," Lakeesha was unable to do so when she was upset and thus her rage cycle (Myles & Southwick, 1999) began, leading to the self-injurious behavior.

Know the student and manage the triggers for these extreme behaviors as best as possible to keep him from losing control. Ask other staff members and parents for a list of known triggers and try to avoid them. However, not all triggers are avoidable, and a systematic method must be implemented to help students who rage (see Chapter Five for a discussion of the rage cycle).

Dealing with Change

Individuals with AS may perceive and react to their environment differently than their neurotypical peers because of a neurological impairment (Frith, 1991). Many exhibit feelings of anxiety and fear through stereotyped behaviors such as repetitive questioning, crying, chewing on hands or shirt, hyperactivity, rocking, or vocal outbursts. When something *unexpected* happens, they will more than likely have difficulty. Indeed, the unexpected can send students with AS into a tailspin or on to a path of rage.

When my son was in the second and third grades, he and my daughter attended private Social Language Groups on Saturday mornings. Every Saturday morning he would pack a bag with his Gameboy™, along with several game cartridges. I allowed him to play the games in the waiting room, as did several other children while waiting for their Social Language Group to begin. Because my two children were in different groups, and there was an hour between their sessions, my son became accustomed to playing the games for the hour before his session. After about four weeks, I noticed that it was becoming increasingly more difficult for him to stop playing the games and go into the room when his Social Language Group was ready to start. As a result, I decided it was time to end this ritual, realizing that the change would be extremely difficult since change does not come easy to him. But I had learned that he could be helped to adjust by (a) giving him a written schedule so he would know what to expect, (b) including some time for him to play the games at a different time during the day, (c) creating a Flexibility Chart with a reward he would really like (see Figure 5.1), and (d) being prepared if his rage cycle began.

I prepared by discussing this change in his routine with the speech-language pathologist to let her know what to expect the following Saturday. I knew my son would react with crying and tantruming when informed that he could not play the games in the waiting room, so I planned to take him jogging up and down the stairs in the building where the speech-language pathologist was located because rigorous physical activity helps diffuse his anger.

As predicted, even though I had shown my son the written schedule, given him the Flexibility Chart, and reviewed and practiced the change several days ahead of time, he had a meltdown. He cried in the car as we drove to the therapist's office, and he verbally refused to cooperate as he kicked the back of my seat in the car. When we arrived at the office, I did not discuss anything with him. I had him jog up the stairs to the second floor, where the office was located. When we entered the office, he dropped to the floor and cried. The speech-language pathologist explained to the others in the waiting room what was happening, as I carried my son to an empty office to cool down. I allowed him to cry and roll around on the floor until he had calmed down. I had made certain that we arrived early enough to allow time for some physical activity. The jog up one flight of stairs when we first arrived was not enough to diffuse his anger. After he had calmed down and was able to talk to me, I told him that it was time for some exercise before his group session. I held his hand, and we walked out of the office to the stairs, where we jogged up and down for about 10 minutes. When he complained about being exhausted, I reminded him that he was earning points on his

Flexibility Chart. That motivated him to keep going. The reward for completing his Flexibility Chart was time at home playing Gameboy, a great motivator!

In social interactions such as playing a game on the playground or having a conversation at lunch, unexpected events or changes in routines often occur that neurotypical children adjust to with ease. However, such unexpected events or changes cause problems for the child with AS. During a kickball game at recess, for example, some children may decide to end the game before the recess period is over and begin playing freeze tag instead. Even though all of the children have smoothly made the transition to the new game, the student with AS usually has difficulty, finding the change abrupt, unexpected, and frustrating, possibly leading to a tantrum, rage, or meltdown (TRM). Likewise, if the student with AS is unable to sit in the seat where she normally sits for lunch, she may begin to have a TRM. Most students would look for another seat or ask the person in the seat to move, but the student with AS often lacks the ability to think flexibly and find a solution to the problem.

Have the student with AS rehearse appropriate responses to change, such as asking to be included in the new game or telling the other children that she would like to continue playing the current game for 5 more minutes before they change. This helps prepare her for such situations. Rehearsal of events that might occur unexpectedly at lunch, such as a fire drill, a public announcement, or being told that there is no talking for 10 minutes, also provides the student with experience in dealing with change. By using a reward system that encourages flexibility in thinking and by rehearsing appropriate behaviors to unexpected changes, the student with AS can learn to deal with change.

If a student becomes difficult to manage, be sure to consult with parents and staff to assess the current support system, appropriateness of interventions and placement, and methods for helping the student learn to adjust to change. Regular team meetings and open communication with staff members and parents help ensure that an individually designed plan for teaching the student to deal with change works (see Chapter Five for a discussion on adjusting to change and difficult moments).

The goal for the student should be to function as well as possible within the classroom. A child who cries every time another student touches his desk needs extra support in order to adjust to the classroom environment. For example, a paraprofessional may act as a social interpreter, explaining to the student with AS that sometimes others will accidentally touch her things. Another way to help is to allow the student with AS to sit apart from the group until she has become accustomed to being close to other students. Set up a desk at the front, back, or side of the room that is not within a group of desks, or put a large trifold board like those used for science fair displays on the student's desk to provide isolation from other students until she is ready to sit with another student. When she has adjusted to being in a room full of children, allow her to do a favorite activity at a table with another student and then with a group of 2-3 students. The teacher or other adult facilitator should be close enough to monitor verbal exchanges, script when necessary, and interpret the neurotypical children's behavior for the student with AS. Over time, most students with AS will become familiar with their peers, the feeling of being in close proximity to many children at once, and adjust to working in a classroom full of children. Students who have difficulty adjusting to the classroom environment where change is inevitable may need an individual study carrel or time outside the classroom in a smaller setting, or in a quiet private area – home base – for part of the day (see Chapter Five).

Many children with AS view the behaviors of others as unexpected and confusing even though the same behaviors seem quite ordinary to the other children and adults at school. Some students with AS need daily assistance in adjusting to all the change that takes place within social situations at school. Remember, these children have an autism spectrum disorder and have difficulty interpreting the actions of others.

Dealing with the social struggles of the student with AS is one of the greatest challenges you will meet in working with these children. This is an area where the speech-language pathologist, social worker, and

Dealing with the social struggles of the student with AS is one of the greatest challenges you will meet.

paraprofessional play a major role. They can assist, coach, and direct the student with AS to help her learn to function successfully within the social climate of the classroom.

Sensory Integration

Many children with Asperger Syndrome have sensory integration problems. Simply stated, their senses are over- (hyper) or under- (hypo) sensitive (see Table 2.3). Any of the senses may be affected. For example, they may be sensitive to loud sounds or certain frequencies, sunlight or fluorescent lighting, or particular scents or odors. Their sensitivities may be so overwhelming and unpleasant that physical pain, nausea, confusion, or headaches results. Reactions to these stimuli may be observed as immature, defiant, or aggressive behavior. In reality, students are feeling anxious, ill, or distressed, and they are reacting to those feelings (Myles, Cook, Miller, Rinner, & Robbins, 2000).

TABLE 2.3
Sensory Characteristics of Children with AS

- Hypo-/hypersensitivity to pain
- Hypo-/hypersensitivity to sounds or particular frequencies
- Hypo-/hypersensitivity to light
- Hypo-/hypersensitivity to touch
- Hypo-/hypersensitivity to taste and/or textures of foods
- Hypo-/hypersensitivity to types of smells

Imagine having a bright light shine directly into your eyes for hours at a time. The discomfort and annoyance you would feel is comparable to what many individuals with AS experience in their everyday exposure to sunlight or certain indoor lighting.

Shauna described the sensations she felt in response to certain stimuli. Some loud sounds made her feel as if someone were scratching her. While riding in the car, the loud, low-frequency sound from the stereo in a nearby car gave her the feeling that someone was scratching her back with sharp fingernails, causing her to pull her shoulders back and squirm around in her seat. Tactile irritations like the seams in her clothing rubbing against her skin caused her to feel nauseous, and the large, fluorescent lights in the supermarket made her anxious and irritable. To the unknowing observer, Shauna's reactions appear irrational and inappropriate. However, to Shauna, they are very real and debilitating.

Understanding the severity of sensory defensiveness in individuals with AS will help teachers and therapists learn how to control some of the triggers that may cause problems for individual students. Table 2.4 shows the location and function of the sensory systems. When overstimulated, my son used to become very hyperactive, running around in circles and jumping on furniture. Over time, we have identified the triggers for this behavior, eliminating them when possible. In addition, we have increased his tolerance for sensory input by slowly exposing him to particular stimuli and by providing practice and rehearsal of appropriate behaviors. Although he stills gets agitated at times and becomes hyperactive, this behavior has been significantly reduced because of the efforts we have made to help him adjust to his environment.

Because the individual with AS does not always process sensory input accurately, she may be hyposensitive (Dunn, Myles, & Orr, 2002), which means that she under-registers sensory events. Such an individual may not pay attention to sound, seem unaware of persons or things in her environment or take longer to respond to certain sensory events. Some children try to counteract these experiences by seeking sensory input. As a result, some children with AS constantly touch or stroke things, put objects in their mouths, chew on clothes or hands, or smell everything in sight. Heather, a 5-year-old with AS, strokes her peers' clothing during circle time and free-choice activities in kindergarten. Most of the girls in her class have become accustomed to this, but as she gets older, her peers will not be so accepting of such behavior. Another girl with AS smells everything new she sees, including odd things such as finger nail clippers and other children's books. Some children may have a combination of both hyper- (too much) and hypo- (too little) sensitivities. For example, it is not uncommon for some children to ignore pain that would generally be considered unbearable by others. However, the presence of a hangnail or a paper cut could be excruciating.

TABLE 2.4
Location and Functions of the Sensory Systems

SYSTEM	LOCATION	FUNCTION
Tactile (touch)	**Skin** – density of cell distribution varies throughout the body. Areas of greatest density include mouth, hands, and genitals.	Provides information about the environment and object qualities (touch, pressure, texture, hard, soft, sharp, dull, heat, cold, pain).
Vestibular (balance)	**Inner ear** – stimulated by head movements and input from other senses, especially visual.	Provides information about where our body is in space, and whether or not we or our surroundings are moving. Tells about speed and direction of movement.
Proprioception (body awareness)	**Muscles and joints** – activated by muscle contractions and movement.	Provides information about where a certain body part is and how it is moving.
Visual (sight)	**Retina of the eye** – stimulated by light.	Provides information about objects and persons. Helps us define boundaries as we move through time and space.
Auditory (hearing)	**Inner ear** – stimulated by air/sound waves.	Provides information about sounds in the environment (loud, soft, high, low, near, far).
Gustatory (taste)	**Chemical receptors in the tongue** – closely entwined with the olfactory (smell) system.	Provides information about different types of taste (sweet, sour, bitter, salty, spicy).
Olfactory (smell)	**Chemical receptors in the nasal structure** – closely associated with the gustatory system.	Provides information about different types of smell (musty, acrid, putrid, flowery, pungent).

From *Asperger Syndrome and Sensory Issues: Practical Solutions for Making Sense of the World* (p. 5), by B. S. Myles, K. T. Cook, N. E. Miller, L. Rinner, & L. A. Robbins, 2000, Shawnee Mission, KS: AAPC. Reprinted with permission.

While walking in a Halloween parade, Beth's classmates noticed a trail of blood dripping from her hand. Earlier, she had tripped on her costume, but she quickly got up and rejoined the parade. She was completely unaware that she had cut her hand in the fall. After the parade, her teacher retraced their path and found the piece of glass that had cut Beth's hand. It was a sliver of a soda bottle, about two inches in diameter. She could not believe that Beth, the girl who can hear a door open at the far end of the school and refuses to touch anything sticky, had not felt a piece of glass slice her hand open.

Cody, a 10-year-old with AS, slowly stopped using his right arm. When this continued for several days, his mother took him to the doctor only to discover that his arm was broken. Cody had fallen out of a tree the week before, but he had failed to tell anyone because the break did not bother him for several days. Even then, it did not bother him enough to do anything other than limit his use of the arm. If you suspect that a student with AS has suffered an injury, be sure to consult with his parents and other professionals to determine the seriousness or severity of the injury and act accordingly.

For many students, a sensory integration evaluation by an occupational therapist may be necessary to provide the information you need to accommodate this student. Figure 2.1 shows sample sensory characteristics of a typical child with AS.

Motor Functioning

Both fine- and gross-motor functioning may be affected in individuals with AS due to neurological problems that make it difficult for them to imitate and execute motor tasks, thereby affecting coordination, timing, and dexterity (see Table 2.5). Although some individuals with AS do not have motor deficits, many experience great difficulty in school, especially with handwriting, note-taking, and physical activities like running and ball games. In the following, we will look more closely at some of these problems.

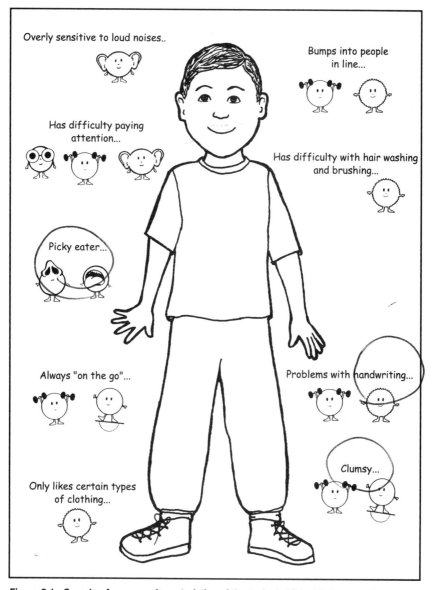

Figure 2.1. Sample of sensory characteristics of the typical child with Asperger Syndrome.

From *Asperger Syndrome and Sensory Issues: Practical Solutions for Making Sense of the World* (p. 5), by B. S. Myles, K. T. Cook, N. E. Miller, L. Rinner, & L. A. Robbins, 2000, Shawnee Mission, KS: AAPC. Reprinted with permission.

TABLE 2.5
Motor Characteristics of Children with AS

- Poor coordination
- Poor balance
- Hypotonia (low muscle tone)
- Dysgraphia (inability to write legibly)
- Poor and/or slow motor planning (timing, imitating, and execution of movements)
- Poor and/or slow visual-motor planning

Fine-Motor Skills

The range in fine-motor impairment is wide – from minimal impairment like incorrect grip or poor letter formation to severe impairment, such as complete dysgraphia (inability to write legibly). Children should not be penalized for having dysgraphia. Instead, they need accommodations that enable them to complete their work, such as a reducing the length of assignments or offering alternative means of displaying their knowledge. This could include verbal responses or having a writing partner (a paraprofessional, student, or parent volunteer) complete the writing portion of an assignment upon dictation of the student with AS.

Handwriting is excruciatingly difficult for many students with AS. When in the primary grades, they may not be able to copy letters correctly, keep up with the rest of the class, and maintain self-control when they feel frustrated. As a result, they may refuse to complete an assignment or lash out in anger. Often, students in upper-elementary grades write like students in kindergarten or first grade, laboring over a task, concentrating all efforts on letter formation, which impedes their ability to focus on the content of their writing. Couple this with sensory processing problems, anxiety, and organizational difficulties, and the student may well be on her way to a TRM.

Keep in mind that this is a disability, not a behavior or attitude problem. The use of a keyboard and assistive technology such as *Alphasmart, Write:OutLoud,* and *Co:Writer* work very well for the student with AS (see Chapter Three) as does modifying assignments to accommodate for this neurological impairment (see Chapter Four). Another way to help children who have handwriting difficulties due to AS is to use Handwriting Without Tears (HWT), a handwriting program created by an occupational therapist and handwriting expert, Jan Olsen (www.hwtears.com). Many teachers and parents have found assistive technology and HWT to be successful tools for children with AS.

In addition to handwriting problems, students with AS experience difficulty cutting, painting, molding clay, gluing, and other tasks that require manual dexterity. This means that they will need assistance with art projects, both in the regular classroom and in art class, and may need modifications in assignments (see Chapter Four). They also tend to have difficulty with visual-motor tasks such as copying information from the board or a screen displaying overhead projections. Likewise, they may have difficulty copying information from books and papers. Visual-motor problems cause them to lose their place, have difficulty completing tasks, and are a source of anxiety.

Difficulties in these areas are particularly troublesome because assessment of proficiency and knowledge of a subject is typically based on written performance (Myles & Adreon, 2001). This can be compared to the international student who is capable of scoring well on tests in his native language but, when required to test in another language, scores much lower even though he has mastered all the necessary skills and learned all the information taught in the class. Another comparison can be made to students with visual impairments. No one would expect a student with a visual impairment to demonstrate his abilities through reading text. When being tested, he would be given Braille or provided assistance to compensate for his disability so that his proficiency and knowledge could be accurately evaluated. Students who have impairments in motor skills are deserving of the same assistance.

Gross-Motor Skills

Gross-motor impairments include lack of coordination and balance, in addition to hypotonia (low muscle tone) of the upper body. Many children with AS experience difficulties in the timing, imitation, and execution of motor tasks and activities. As a result, they may have trouble participating in gym class or recess activities. They need direct instruction and extra practice in order to master many motor skills or participate in certain activities. For example, adaptive P.E. accommodations such as direct, private instruction in ball skills and game rules have proven very successful for many. When writing the IEP, be sure to incorporate motor skill goals and include the school occupational therapist, physical therapist, physical education teacher, and adaptive P.E. teacher in writing the goals.

My son's P.E. teacher was extremely instrumental in evaluating his motor performance as well as designing an alternative plan that included a modified curriculum, a paraprofessional to assist him during the regular P.E. class, and one-on-one time with an occupational therapist and adaptive P.E. teacher to instruct him in the following skills: catching and throwing a variety of balls, kicking stationary and moving balls, dribbling a basketball, hopping on one foot, jumping with both feet, alternating feet while jumping, jumping rope, skipping, walking on a balance beam, and running. In addition, the P.E. teacher modified goals and adjusted expectations to fit his specific needs and abilities. For example, since it was determined during the end-of-the-year assessment that he cannot run the same distance as the other children in the class, he now runs a shorter distance in the same time period. This modification makes it possible for him to participate with the rest of the class, feel good about himself by not finishing the task so far behind the other children, and at the same time, work on developing his motor skills.

The difficulties children with AS face due to their poor motor skills can create numerous problems for them each day. Due to what appears as clumsiness and awkwardness, they are often teased and ostracized, and as a result feel humiliated, embarrassed, and depressed. The occupational therapist, physical therapist, physical education teacher, social worker, speech-language pathologist, and parents can all work with the teacher to provide the support the student will need, which includes a developmental program for building strength and endurance as well as teaching fine- and gross-motor planning activities, assistance during physical activities, opportunities for practicing and refining motor skills, and individual accommodations/modifications within the classroom.

Cognitive Processing

The degree and type of impairment in cognitive processing varies greatly among individuals with AS. Although the average IQ of individuals with AS is 100, the range of intelligence is wide, spanning from below average to very superior. While it is difficult to discern patterns in the cognitive functioning of persons with AS because of their range in abilities, Table 2.6 lists some of the cognitive characteristics associated with Asperger Syndrome.

TABLE 2.6
Cognitive Processing Characteristics of Children with AS

- Rigidity in thinking and routine
- Difficulty perceiving danger
- Overselectivity to information or stimuli
- Narrow and/or intense focus of interest
- Impulsivity
- Difficulty with executive functions (planning, prioritizing, organizing)
- Difficulty discerning between fiction and reality
- Stereotyped, repetitive, and/or ritualistic behaviors
- Difficulty interpreting multimodal information
- Hyperlexia
- Difficulty retrieving experiential memories

Children with AS do not always perceive the world like their neurotypical peers. Many have difficulty discerning fact from fiction and/or recognizing danger. They may not be able to focus on the "big picture" but instead over-focus on particular features. These children may walk right into a busy street, focusing on a leaf they see in the middle of the road, oblivious to the traffic around them. To complicate matters, they have trouble shifting attention when something has caught their interest. As a result, if you ask them to change activities or stop without a warning to do so, you may be met with resistance.

As in all groups of children, students with AS demonstrate a variety of learning problems and abilities. In the following, we will look at the more common, including

- theory of mind deficits
- difficulties with executive functions
- rigidity in thinking
- impulsivity
- memory problems
- learning disabilities
- hyperlexia
- possession of superior strengths

Theory of Mind

Many individuals with AS have difficulty with perspective-taking. This means that they are not able to see things from any other perspective than their own. Known as a theory of mind deficit, this makes it difficult, if not impossible, for a person with AS to think about what somebody else might be thinking.

For example, Jake, a neurotypical student, tells Anna, a student with AS, that he thinks his dog may have eaten his homework. Other students in close proximity hear what Jake just said and begin to laugh. Anna, on the other hand, asks Jake if his dog is OK after eating paper. Jake shrugs his shoulders and replies, "No, he died! The homework was too much for him!" with a big grin on his face. Again the other students laugh. Anna is now completely confused. Jake points to her, laughs, and walks away. Anna did not realize that her initial reaction prompted Jake to exaggerate his story. Anna became the joke because she could not think about what the others were thinking. Jake, on the other hand, knew Anna was thinking about the horrible ordeal she thought the dog was experiencing, and was able to use that information. Because Anna was only able to hear Jake's words and not think about what he might be thinking, she was left confused, and completely misunderstood what Jake was really saying and doing.

Another theory of mind problem can occur when a student with AS fails to consider what the teacher *really* means when she says something. For example, one day while I was leading my third-grade class down the hall toward our classroom, I turned back to them and whispered, "Yes!" They all smiled. They all knew I was pleased with their behavior in the hall because they were walking quietly without disturbing each other or any of the classes that we passed. They all knew what I was thinking except one student – a student with AS. Walking near the front of the line, he asked me, "Yes, what, Ms. Moore?" He was not able to discern that I was thinking about the behavior of the class and had responded positively to it. When I looked back at him and smiled, he continued to look at me, waiting for an answer. It did not occur to him that I was thinking about what he had been thinking and that it brought a smile to my face. At that point I explained to him why I had whispered "Yes" to the class. He nodded his head in agreement and went to his seat.

When my son was in second grade he would follow the teacher all over the room, asking her questions as she tried to assist other students. He was unable to read her body language and unable to think about what she must be thinking about him following her around all the time. As a result, he was completely confused the first time she told him to sit down without answering his questions. He thought she did not like him and was ignoring him. The teacher cleverly created a hand signal to remind my son to think about his behavior, and he has now learned to think about when it would be appropriate to approach the teacher to ask a question. He still struggles with this, but because of the time and effort his second-grade teacher took to teach him to think about what others might be thinking, he has been able to improve his ability to take others' perspective.

Many students with AS do or say things that teachers and other students find annoying or humorous, depending on the situation. They are not trying to be annoying or funny. They are simply unable to know what others are thinking and lack the ability to adjust their own thinking, words, and actions accordingly.

Executive Functions

Planning, prioritizing, and organizing skills, also known as executive functions, are affected in many individuals with AS. In school, executive function difficulties become apparent when students are expected to keep track of their belongings, manage multiple-step assignments, or complete tasks in a timely manner. Students with AS often lose their supplies, have a messy desk, and turn in late or incomplete work. In addition, many have trouble starting and stopping tasks and activities. Despite a great need for order and control, they are unable to achieve it on their own. They are not lazy and careless but lack the cognitive ability to self-monitor and think flexibly.

A teacher unfamiliar with the problems inherent in AS may find it difficult to understand why an otherwise bright, highly verbal student is unable to maintain any sense of order at school and may reprimand the student instead of implementing a support system. Written outlines of expectations and assignment tasks and frequent checking on the student to help her reorganize and monitor her progress can be effective supports. Given appropriate strategies that assist with planning, prioritizing, and organizing, students with AS can function quite successfully (see Chapter Three for specific strategies).

One of the hallmark traits of AS is a narrow and/or intense focus on a particular interest. For example, students may spend several hours a day reading and learning about a particular topic, often finding it difficult to focus on anything else. Likewise, they may become over-focused on the details of an assignment. One student with AS spent an entire test period aligning answers on the page, and as a result failed to complete the test on time. Unable to shift his attention to the task at hand, he failed a test on material that he had, indeed, mastered. Because of their problems with over-selectivity and rigid thinking, children with AS need careful monitoring and redirection to ascertain that they are still on task and performing up to their potential.

> *One of the hallmark traits of AS is a narrow and/or intense focus on a particular interest.*

Rigidity in Thinking

Individuals with AS are rigid thinkers – things are either black or white, right or wrong, logical or illogical. As a result, it is often difficult to get them to think outside their own beliefs or perceptions (Attwood, 1998). One of the most important skills a child with AS can learn is to be FLEXIBLE! Children learn to adjust to unexpected changes when change is introduced into the schedule in a systematic and planned way. Those who are never taught how to deal with change will have great difficulty both in school and in social situations. (See Chapter Five for ideas on how to teach students to deal with change.)

Impulsivity

Another problem common in students with AS is impulsivity. Most children learn to control their impulses. For example, if a neurotypical child, seated in class, looks over to the door and notices a friend walking by in the hall, he does not yell out from his seat, "Hi, Josh!" He controls himself in accordance with the rules and expectations of the classroom by waiting until recess to talk to his friend. However, the child with AS might jump out of her chair and scream, "Hey, I know him! That's my neighbor. He lives next door to me. Hi, Josh!" Needless to say, such impulsivity can be very disruptive. Written rules for behavior and practice will help to remedy this kind of problem.

Memory Problems

Some individuals with AS have incredible rote memory, yet have difficulty with meaningful memory. For example, they may be able to tell you every item discovered on the ocean floor at the site where the sunken Titanic was discovered, but not be able to recall how the disaster impacted the world, as explained in an article they read in their social studies book. They need assistance in locking information into memory and in accessing that information. It is as if their brain cannot process information unless it is presented in list format; and similarly, it can only give it back in list format. Students with AS may need additional time and visuals to process the pertinent information given in a reading assignment. It may also help if the information is presented in short blocks of time over several days with frequent review, rather than all at once in one long session.

Students with AS also have difficulty applying newly learned skills in real-life situations and learning to adhere to social rules that other students acquire quickly and with ease. This means that social rules explained and taught in isolation (e.g., in a therapy session with a speech-language pathologist or a social worker) often do not transfer to real-life situations. A common practice in working with students with AS is to teach them a social rule like "Wait your turn in line" in a one-on-one session with an adult. The student with AS can repeat the rule, list the situations in which she must apply the rule, but walk right out the therapist's office and into the classroom and forget to wait for her turn to go to an activity. In order to apply what she is learning in isolation, this student needs adult intervention, visual reminders, and prompts that are not faded until the skill or rule is mastered. Frequent and repeated practice of newly learned tasks, skills, and behaviors will help transfer them to students' long-term, meaningful memory.

Learning Disabilities

As within any group of children, students with AS demonstrate a range of ability. Some have learning disabilities in addition to AS. Some are identified as gifted and talented, while others are gifted in some areas and have a learning disability in another. As a result, these children not only need accommodations for their problems due to AS, they also need strategies to help them compensate for their learning difficulties. This may include a reading disorder (dyslexia or hyperlexia), mathematics disorder, or expressive and/or receptive language disorders.

To meet the needs of children with AS, it is important to accurately determine the cause of their academic problems. What may look like a learning disability may be a problem due to AS and vice versa. For example, a writing problem may be due to an actual learning disability or it may be the result of hypotonia, poor motor planning, or sensory issues due to AS. The methods for accommodating and remediating a writing problem due to a learning disability are different from those used for a writing problem due to hypotonia and poor motor planning. For example, if a student has difficulty writing because she has dyslexia, she needs a comprehensive reading/writing program that focuses on developing reading/writing skills for students with dyslexia and should be taught

Careful and accurate assessment and a well-designed educational plan are essential. by a reading specialist. However, the student who has writing difficulties due to hypotonia and poor motor planning needs a program developed by an occupational therapist that helps improve upper-body strength, fine-motor skills, and motor-planning proficiency so that she is able to write using a pen, pencil, or keyboard while seated at a desk. Careful and accurate assessment and a well-designed educational plan are essential to meet each student's specific needs.

Hyperlexia

Another problem experienced by many children with AS is hyperlexia. That is, they have the ability to decode text at a very young age but do not comprehend at the same level. For example, you may have a 6-year-old student reading at the fifth-grade level based on an assessment of his oral reading. However, upon assessment of his comprehension, you find that he comprehends at a first-grade level. A student who is hyperlexic may be able to read aloud (or word call) a geography book or novel but fail to understand what he has read. Therefore, it is imperative to evaluate comprehension in order to provide the appropriate level of work for the student. (See Chapter Four for information on evaluating and teaching reading comprehension.)

Superior Strengths

Some children with AS exhibit superior strengths or talents and therefore need to be appropriately challenged in the areas where they are gifted. Several inventions, discoveries, and works of art have been made by people with AS or those who manifest characteristics of AS. These scientists and artists were original thinkers with unique interests and abilities: a scientist who changed the world with his discoveries, a musician who wrote masterpiece after masterpiece that endured the test of time, and a professor who has published numerous papers and books on a particular culture in a faraway land.

43

It is interesting to note that many educators and psychologists have identified a set of behaviors that are typical of gifted individuals that are now being identified as traits in individuals with Asperger Syndrome. Winner (1996) provides descriptions of gifted children, including the following characteristics and traits:

- Long attention span
- Large vocabulary and large store of verbal knowledge
- Unusually intense reactions to noise, pain, frustration
- Persistent questioning
- High energy level
- Obsessive interests
- Prodigious memory
- Logical reasoning
- Handwriting difficulties
- Social difficulties
- Preferences for friends who are older
- Excellent sense of humor
- Interest in philosophical and moral issues
- Independent abilities: gifted in some areas but not in others

You may have a student who can recite the names of every U.S. president, his place of birth, and years in office, but the same student has no friends. He sits alone at recess reading his book about the presidents. It is obvious that he is bright, but he lacks the skills to interact with his peers. What does the future hold for such a child when so many jobs require interpersonal communication skills and proficiency at social interactions? For some, their social and linguistic impairments have so greatly affected their lives that they are unable to hold jobs or finish school, despite their special gifts. How sad to think that some of these individuals never reach their potential.

A number of schools sponsor science, chess, environmental, and history clubs where students with AS can explore and develop their special interests, and others offer after-school music clubs where students get together to practice their instruments. In the school where I taught, we offered a before-school language program to interested students. Some children with AS are skilled at learning foreign languages and this special language program provided a time for them to explore their interest while interacting with neurotypical children. If you recognize and nurture their talents and provide them with appropriate interventions and support, students with AS have the potential to make astonishing achievements. All have the potential to find fulfillment and happiness along the way.

The cognitive characteristics of children with AS are numerous and complex. Some have learning disabilities, many have difficulties with theory of mind and executive functions, and some have superior strengths. Each child with AS is different and should be treated as an individual.

"Treat people as if they were
what they ought to be and
you help them to become what
they are capable of being."

JOHANN W. VON GOETHE

CHAPTER THREE

Organizational Accommodations

D ue to their language, social, sensory, motor, and cognitive difficulties, students with AS need accommodations designed to meet their unique needs. These include organizing the learning environment, grouping and managing students for cooperative work projects, creating and using visual aids, priming (Wilde, Koegel & Koegel, 1992), using assistive technology, teaching note-taking techniques, modifying student presentations, developing an assignment notebook and homework routine, and modifying assessments. The strategies described in this chapter offer structure and predictability for students with AS, which help enable them to develop a routine, keep themselves organized, and meet teacher expectations (Myles & Adreon, 2001) – important skills necessary for success at school.

Classroom Organization

Providing a successful learning environment requires specific preparation and planning. One of the best accommodations you can provide for students with AS is an organized and predictable classroom setting (Attwood, 1998; Myles & Simpson, 1998). Change and clutter may result in anxiety, behavior problems, repeated questioning, and/or withdrawal.

At the beginning of the school year, provide the student with a map of the school and the classroom and help orient her. The student may need to carry the map with her for days or weeks depending on the severity of the disability. Familiarity with and predictability of the surroundings provide a sense of comfort and security.

Familiarity with and predictability of the surroundings provide a sense of comfort and security.

Physical Arrangement

Children with AS often have difficulty with balance and coordination, as well as visual-spatial perception, so a simple room design works best. Arrange desks in groups of four to five to keep the child from becoming overwhelmed.

Many children with AS prefer not to sit in the middle of a group because they feel people are invading their personal space, which makes them uncomfortable. Therefore, whenever possible, seat students with AS at the end of a row. Also, as mentioned, many individuals with AS have *hypotonia*, a decrease in tone that results in weakness in the muscles. Since it typically affects just the upper body, it makes it particularly difficult to sit on seats without backs. When students are required to sit on risers, during music class or at assemblies, for example, offer the student with AS frequent breaks to get up and move around before sitting down again.

Students with AS, as well as students with attention deficit disorder (ADD) or attention deficit hyperactivity disorder (ADHD), may have trouble focusing in a room covered in posters, signs, pictures, and so on. Help maintain the students' attention on the teacher and lesson by keeping the room simply decorated. Objects, art projects, and signs hanging from overhead lights can be very distracting. If possible, do not hang objects over the desk of a student with AS. When the students are required to navigate around the room to work at centers or workstations, give the student with AS a map and schedule of her routine and make her route easy to navigate. For example, she may begin at her desk where she completes seat work, followed by a rotation to centers in a clockwise order around the periphery of the room rather than having to cross the room several times, weaving in and out of desks to move from center to center.

Because children with AS function best in a structured and predictable environment, it is best to post class rules, calendars, bathroom passes, and schedules in the same location for the entire school year. Clearly label each bulletin board, workstation, reading corner, and so on, with a sign and make sure each section of the room has clear, definable boundaries (Cumine, Leach, & Stevenson, 1998).

Color Coding

Color coding is a great organizational tool, not only for the child with AS but for the entire class. Keep all signs, folders, and containers for a particular subject uniform in color. For example, if red is for reading, the students have red folders for keeping reading packets, quizzes, notes, and so forth. You may also use a red sign to label the reading corner or the class library. Similarly, if blue is the color for science, then all containers, folders, and bins in the science corner are blue. In one school, the entire student body used the same color-code system. As the students progressed through the grades, they knew that red was the reading color, yellow was the color for their take-home folders, blue was for math, and so on. In this way, all students were helped to stay organized, not only the student with AS.

Even though it is important to have a classroom that is organized, structured, and predictable, it is important to remind students that ***THINGS DO CHANGE!*** Be sure to have a sign in the room that reminds the student with AS that things may change. This may be a sign on her desk, a sentence at the end of each checklist or activity schedule, or a note card that the child keeps in a pocket such as a Change in Routine Card (see Figure 3.1).

Change in Routine

NOTICE: _____ will be changed

on _____ because _____

_____

The new _____

is _____

Figure 3.1. Change in routine card.

If a change in the room set-up or learning environment is necessary, be sure to advise the student with AS before making the change and use the Change in Routine Card to indicate that a change will be taking place. This will help alleviate some of the anxiety the student feels as a result of change in the environment. A little warning goes a long way in helping students deal with change! What seems like a minor adjustment to the teacher or other students may be the source of great anger and frustration for children with Asperger Syndrome.

Grouping Students

In most classrooms, the seating arrangements vary depending on the activity or the routine for the day. Some students with AS should be permitted to sit alone because close proximity to others may be so anxiety-producing or distracting that it impedes learning, or because they do not have the social skills to sit with a group. Provide opportunities for peer interaction, but do not force it. With this in mind, it is also important to be accepting and respectful of the student's personal space when individuals with AS distance themselves from others. This is often a coping strategy, not a display of defiance or disinterest. At times, a student with AS will move his desk, chair, or body away from whomever he is seated near, typically when it is a new seating arrangement such as in a group activity, when the desks have been moved, during a reading group, or during one of the special classes like art or music. What is happening is that the student is being placed in a new situation that causes him to feel uncomfortable, nervous, and/or anxious. To the neurotypical person, these feelings may seem irrational. However, this is truly an uncomfortable situation for the individual with AS, who needs time to adjust to and deal with these feelings.

When the student with AS is comfortable sitting with others, arrange desks in small groups as previously mentioned. Try to keep the student seated next to the same student or students for at least a month or two. This serves a dual purpose: predictability *and* friendship opportunities. Also keep in mind that the student with AS should be seated so that he is oriented in the direction that he needs to face for instruction from the teacher.

Cooperative Work

Keep grouping for cooperative work flexible. Match the student with AS with another student who possesses complementary abilities. For example, if the student with AS is talented at drawing, pair her with a student who is good at writing. Or, if the student has a talent for storytelling but lacks fine-motor coordination, pair her with a student who has good penmanship. Working together on a project provides opportunities for social skills practice such as turn-taking, conversation, sharing of interests, and cooperation, in addition to working on the intended concept and skills for the lesson.

Keep grouping for cooperative work flexible.

Groups may also be formed based on a special interest of the student with AS. Special interests are great motivators for encouraging participation and boosting self-esteem (Gagnon, 2001; Willey, 1999). For example, if the students are to work in pairs to research a particular animal or culture and later present their findings to the whole class, allow the student with AS to do research in the area of her special interest and pair her with someone who would work well with her – either someone who shares a similar interest or someone who is able to work cooperatively with the student with AS. For example, if the students are studying ancient cultures and you know that the student with AS is fascinated with the Titanic, her special interest can be used to motivate her. Since the Titanic was built and used during modern times, the student would not be able to do her research project on the people of 1912 in England and Ireland. She would, however, be able to link her special interest to the people of Pompei who perished in the ashes from the eruption of Mt. Vesuvius. Connect the disastrous sinking of the Titanic to the tragic loss of life in Pompei – both unexpected and important historical events. Further connect it by having the student research how modern technology was used to uncover the remains of the culture in Pompei and the remains from the Titanic at the bottom of the Atlantic Ocean. By linking her interest in the Titanic to the people of Pompei, the student with AS can use her interest to cooperate and participate in the group project. The objectives of this lesson are to develop cooperative learning skills, an understanding of ancient cultures, and skills needed to organize information to present to the class. Because the student with AS is able to be motivated to work on this project using her special interest, she is able to meet the learning objectives. This group project also provides an excellent opportunity for the student to shine in an area in which she feels confident.

Remember, if the student lacks social skills, cooperative group activities may lead to big problems! Therefore, be flexible in your expectations and in the way you arrange groups to minimize problems for everyone in the class. For instance, do not allow students to choose their own partners. Almost every student I have met who has AS has told me that she or he is rarely chosen as a partner or group member when the decision is left up to the students. Rotate partners as needed, giving all the children opportunities to work with several of their classmates, rather than just their friends. Get to know their personalities, strengths, and difficulties, as well as the dynamics of their relationships.

Assign groups for specific reasons, and plan the groups according to the role you want the child to experience or the relationship you want to foster. For example, if the student with AS has been working in social skills training on giving up control, pair her with a leader to whom she will have to relinquish some control in order to complete an activity. Although she will need adult supervision, scripting, and guidance, she will have the experience of taking direction from someone else rather than being the one to make all the decisions, as would occur if paired with a student who is typically a follower. Similarly, for the student with AS who is trying to develop a friendship with one of her classmates, pair her with that student so they will have the topic of the assignment or project to use as a basis for starting a conversation. It is easier for a student with AS to discuss topics related to school in a formal situation than personal topics in informal situations such as in the hall, at recess, or at lunch. This kind of careful pairing will help the student develop confidence in her ability to communicate with a peer and provide her the opportunity to work on a group project with someone with whom she feels comfortable.

Visuals

Have you ever noticed that some students forget the rules when you have a substitute teacher and that others forget the routine after a long weekend or the winter break? Usually, a few verbal reminders are all that is needed to get the class back on track again. Like most students, children with AS need reminders – only much more frequently. You may find yourself repeatedly reminding students with AS about rules, steps for a task, where supplies are located, and so on. Some may need to be reminded on a daily basis.

Visual aids are one of the best strategies for dealing with this problem. Because of the difficulties students with AS have in processing multiple pieces of auditory information, written schedules and checklists are much more effective than constant verbal reminders.

Children with communication problems require less, not more verbalization (Quill, 1995). Giving them a written list of instructions helps them by reducing the number of verbal reminders needed and increases independence.

> **Many students cannot work independently without visual cues.**

Many students cannot work independently without visual cues, needing them on a daily basis to stay on track. Provide visual aids for all new activities and tasks as well as for regular daily activities. For a detailed discussion on how to design visual supports, see *Making Visual Supports Work in the Home and Community: Strategies for Individuals with Autism and Asperger Syndrome* (Savner & Myles, 2000).

Without visual aids, some students engage in behaviors such as hand-flapping, spinning, and repeated questioning. Others will sit at their desk doing nothing (McClannahan & Krantz, 1999), while yet others will spend too much time focusing on the steps of the task and forget to complete the entire activity. Visual aids benefit the teacher as well as the student by preventing off-task behavior, thereby enabling the teacher to teach and the student to learn.

In the following discussion, we will look at a wide variety of visuals designed for specific purposes to help students with AS function successfully and independently at home, school and in the community.

Daily Schedules

Posting of the daily routine is helpful for all children, and essential for children with AS. The familiarity and predictability it conveys helps create a sense of security and therefore reduces anxiety. Post the schedule in the same location every day.

One way to create a daily schedule is to use laminated cards with magnets on the back. Each card has a subject or activity written on it and can be posted on the chalkboard with the corresponding time or activity number written in chalk. You may also want to give a copy of the schedule to the students to keep in their desks and/or take home at the end of the day. Besides helping the student, this is an easy way to let parents know what happened at school each day and also provides a visual for the parent to use with the child to facilitate communication (see Figure 3.2 for a sample daily schedule).

```
┌─────────────────────────────────────────────────┐
│                                                 │
│   Today is Monday, April 16, 2000               │
│                                                 │
│   Attendance                      8:15          │
│   Math                        8:20 - 9:00       │
│   Reading and Centers        9:00 - 10:00       │
│   Spelling                  10:00 - 10:15       │
│   Writing                   10:15 - 10:45       │
│   *Assembly*                10:45 - 11:30       │
│   Lunch & Recess            11:30 - 12:15       │
│   Music                     12:30 - 1:15        │
│   Science                    1:15 - 1:50        │
│   Read Aloud                 1:50 - 2:20        │
│   Journal                    2:10 - 2:25        │
│   Get Ready to Go                 2:25          │
│   Bell Rings                      2:30          │
│                                                 │
│      * SOMETIMES  THE  SCHEDULE  CHANGES *      │
└─────────────────────────────────────────────────┘
```

Figure 3.2. Daily schedule.

A great peer activity for the student with AS is to have him post the daily schedule on the chalkboard with another student. First, the teacher needs to provide several cards labeled with subjects, break times, and special activities. If you are using laminated cards with magnets on the back, it is easy for the student with AS to put them on the chalkboard. The partner's job is to write the time for each activity or subject. At times, it is best to list only the name of the subjects and activities and omit any reference to time because some students with AS watch the clock all day when they are anxious. In this case, the job of the partner is to check the order of the subjects and activities being put on the board to be certain it is correct. The benefit of this activity is twofold for the student with AS: (a) he gains experience working with a neurotypical peer *and*

(b) his level of anxiety for the day is lessened because he is involved in posting the schedule.

For students who cannot read, a picture schedule can be made using photos. To make this type of daily schedule, take photos of the student doing each lesson and activity and display them as you would a written schedule so that they appear in the order that the activities or lessons of the day will occur. These photos can be used in the peer activity described above by having the student work with a peer to help arrange the pictures for each lesson and activity in the correct order for the day.

An important addition to the daily schedule is the phrase: *Sometimes The Schedule Changes*. Write this in bold letters in a color different from the rest of the schedule and put it near the schedule. Another way to make this important statement more notable is to write it on brightly colored paper, laminate it, and attach magnets to the back so it can be posted with the schedule or moved around to indicate a change. Changes and surprises can result in inappropriate behavior, high anxiety, and TRMs. Inevitably, there will be times when you are not able to forewarn students about changes to the schedule; but whenever possible, let the student with AS know when there are going to be changes in the daily routine.

Checklists

Checklists provide predictability and structure for students with AS and help them stay focused so they can complete tasks and assignments. Checklists are visual aids that provide a list of tasks to be performed. They may be a series of pictures or a list of instructions, depending on the student's reading level. Checklists can be printed on colored paper to help the student stay organized and independent. If green is the color you choose for science, for example, then print the checklists for science on green paper. Students may staple the checklist to their work, preventing lost lists and making them serve as a handy reminder.

At first, it is best to make the checklist as detailed as possible. This does not imply using long, wordy sentences. The important thing is that all steps involved in completing a task are included. As you get to know the student better, and as the student becomes familiar with routine activities and tasks, lists can be shortened. If the task is a long assignment, such as writing a multiple-paragraph essay, you may choose to divide it into smaller tasks by having the student complete a checklist for each paragraph in the essay. Remember to adjust the length of assignments and expectations to the appropriate level for the individual student. Many students with AS have trouble completing writing assignments and perform better if provided with a checklist for each step in the writing process. Reducing the length of the finished product or extending the due date may also help, depending on the student's need.

One third-grade teacher found that using a morning checklist (which included all the steps in the morning routine from hanging up coats to filling out the assignment notebook) worked well for a student with AS. Every morning the teacher placed the checklist on the student's desk, prior to his arrival. Figure 3.3 shows an example of a morning checklist.

Morning checklist for _____	
Today's date is _____	
Hang up coat	_____
Empty backpack on desk	_____
Put lunch in lunch cart	_____
Put books in desk	_____
Put folders in desk	_____
Hang backpack on hook	_____
Empty take-home folder on desk	_____
Put homework papers in bin	_____
Open up assignment notebook	_____
Put pencil on desk	_____
Ask teacher to sign assignment notebook	_____
Write homework in assignment notebook	_____
You are now ready to start your day!	

Figure 3.3. Morning checklist.

Each morning, the student would follow the directions on the checklist and put a checkmark next to each task as he completed it. Shortly after, the teacher and/or paraprofessional would check the list to see that the student had, in fact, completed his morning routine. If the student forgot one of the steps, the teacher or paraprofessional circled it so as to prompt the student to finish it. Using the morning checklist, the student was able to stay focused, refrain from disturbing others, and develop some independence. As the student learns the morning routine, this prompt can often be faded, but some students with AS may need it throughout elementary school. For the younger student who is not yet reading, a picture schedule of the morning routine may be used. To make a picture schedule, take photos of the child doing each step in the routine and use them to create the checklist.

Checklists may be used for a variety of purposes. In addition to helping a student follow a routine, they help stay on task and complete all the required steps, such as in a reading assignment for social studies where the student must read a section in a textbook and answer questions related to the reading. The reading checklist in Figure 3.4 can be used for all types of reading assignments, and is useful to both the student and the teacher because it includes space for the student to list difficult vocabulary and/or questions and serves as a record of progress on an assignment.

Checklists may be used for a variety of purposes.

Most teachers and children are unaffected by the noise of shuffling papers, dropping pencils, chairs sliding on the floor, or moving bodies as occurs when the class prepares to go to lunch. However, for the student with AS, who is often very sensitive to sights and sounds, this can be very anxiety-producing, unnerving, distracting, confusing, or even anger-provoking. As a result, he may begin to engage in repetitive behaviors, shut down, or have a TRM. A visual aid such as a checklist will help keep the student focused. Figure 3.5 is an example of a checklist for a transition from math to lunch. As simple as it looks, this checklist helps manage the student during a time that is often distracting, noisy, and chaotic.

Reading Checklist

Name _____ Date _____

Book title: _____

Pages to read: _____

Questions to answer: _____

_____

_____

_____

Difficult words: _____   _____

_____   _____

_____   _____

I have read the assigned pages: YES _____ NO _____

I have answered all of the questions: YES _____ NO _____

I need help with these questions: _____

_____

_____

_____

I stapled the checklist to my paper: YES _____ NO _____

Figure 3.4. Reading checklist.

```
┌─────────────────────────────────────────────┐
│                                             │
│           Get Ready for Lunch               │
│                                             │
│   1. Put books in desk              _____ │
│                                             │
│   2. Put math papers in blue math folder  _____ │
│                                             │
│   3. Put pencils in pencil case     _____ │
│                                             │
│   4. Get lunch from backpack        _____ │
│                                             │
│   5. Sit at desk                    _____ │
│                                             │
│   6. Look at teacher and wait       _____ │
│                                             │
│   7. When the teacher calls my name,        │
│      give her this paper and get in line  _____ │
│                                             │
└─────────────────────────────────────────────┘
```

Figure 3.5. Transition checklist.

Checklists enable students to follow a set sequence of steps every time they perform a task, regardless of who is teaching or assisting them. In other words, checklists provide the consistency and routine that helps the student with AS function well at school.

Activity Plan

The Activity Plan, another visual aid that allows the student to gain independence and develop confidence, is a booklet that lists step-by-step instructions for participating in an activity such as would take place during cooperative work, math lessons, art projects, indoor recess, or free-choice time after completion of a given assignment. The Activity Plan lists what is needed to get started on an activity, includes the steps necessary to stay engaged in the activity, and specifically tells the student to stop when the activity is completed or when the designated time period ends. Booklets should contain only one activity with pictures or words to explain each step, depending on the child's level of language.

A quick and easy way to make an Activity Plan booklet is to use white 8.5" x 11" paper, stack a few sheets together, fold them in half and staple along the folded edge. If the activity booklet is used in a content area such as math, make sure it corresponds in color to that area. If the color code for math is blue, use a marker to draw a band of blue across the top of the booklet. The name of the activity goes on the front of the booklet, and each page contains one step of the activity. Write or type only on the right-hand side of the page to help keep it simple.

Some children have trouble when both the right- and left-hand pages of the booklet contain writing. Be sure to number each step to keep the student on track and to teach sequencing skills.

Finally, develop a system for keeping track of completed steps. You can use a checklist that the student completes or a predetermined number of markers or stickers that corresponds to the number of steps in the activity. For example, when my son was 7 years old, he wrote a check next to each step in the activity booklet to help him keep track of all the steps he needed to complete to play a computer game: turn on the computer, locate the disc, insert the disc, type in your name when prompted on the screen, play the computer game until told to end the game, remove the disc, and put away the disc. I recommend laminating the pages in the Activity Plan booklet and using a washable marker when students write directly in the booklet so it can be used repeatedly.

Another boy with AS uses markers when building puzzles. He is given an Activity Plan that includes the following steps:

1. Choose a puzzle from the puzzle shelf.
2. Take the puzzle to your seat.
3. Open the puzzle box.
4. Build the puzzle.
5. Ask a friend to look at your puzzle.
6. Put the puzzle pieces back in the box.
7. Put the top on the box.
8. Put the puzzle box on the puzzle shelf.

He is also given eight small plastic Digimon™ characters that he places in a container after completing each step of the activity. By using the same number of markers (eight) as the number of steps in the activity (eight), the student knows to stop when all markers are gone. For this to work, the student must first be taught to stop when the pieces are gone. This can be accomplished by practicing the routine with the Activity Plan and the markers in a 1:1 situation until he has mastered it independently. Once this has been mastered, allow him to follow the plan and use his markers independently.

An Activity Plan for building with Legos™ may look like the one illustrated in Table 3.6.

TABLE 3.6
Activity Plan: Steps for Building with Legos™

1. Take the Legos container from the toy shelf, and put it on your desk.
2. Build a vehicle with your Legos.
3. Ask a classmate to look at your Legos.
4. Take apart the Legos.
5. Put the Legos in the container.
6. Put the container on the toy shelf.
7. Put this Activity Plan in the activity folder.

The complexity and level of the activity should match the student's reading ability as well as cognitive and motor abilities. It is important to incorporate as many of the target skills for the student as possible, offering practice and reinforcement of appropriate behavior and opportunities for skill mastery. For example, the Legos activity incorporates many skills including: following directions, reading, problem-solving, social interaction, eye-hand coordination, self-direction.

An Activity Plan for an intermediate-level math activity may include the steps shown in Table 3.7.

TABLE 3.7
Activity Plan: Tangrams™

1. Ask your partner to work at your desk.
2. Go to the math center and get one package of Tangrams.
3. Open the Tangram booklet and choose one of the shapes to copy.
4. Work with your partner to create the shape with the Tangram pieces.
5. Now it is your partner's turn to choose a shape to copy. Ask your partner to choose a shape.
6. Work with your partner to create the shape with the Tangram pieces.
7. Put the Tangram pieces and Tangram booklet back in the bag.
8. Ask your partner to return the Tangram bag to the math center.
9. Put this activity book in the activity folder.

Option Cards

Option Cards are used when the student is having difficulty participating in activities or performing tasks due to sensory defensiveness, anxiety, lack of social skills, and so on, that may cause inappropriate behaviors or reactions. Option Cards serve as a preventive measure as well as a coping strategy that students with AS can learn to use in order to calm their senses, reduce their anxiety, and eliminate their feelings of frustration as they learn to control their emotions.

Option Cards are easy to make on index cards. (For students who are fearful of accepting a modification that makes them look different, a card the size of a business card or trading card is often more acceptable.) The Option Card offers two replacement choices to help the student deal with difficult moments. Write a feeling word or statement across the top of the card such as ANGRY or IT IS TOO LOUD IN HERE. Now write two acceptable options for the student to choose if and when he feels angry or needs to leave the room, such as *I can go to my home base and read a book for 10 minutes or I will jump on my trampoline for 5 minutes before I say anything.*

For students who are not yet reading, cut out or draw two pictures as options such as a picture of a beanbag chair and a picture of a book. Photos of the child doing the options can also be glued to the Option Card. After writing down or drawing the options (you may want to include the student in making them), laminate the cards and place them in a white pocket folder. Write OPTION CARDS on the front and tell the student to keep the folder in his desk.

When a student with AS becomes anxious or agitated, he may not be able to recognize that he needs to use an Option Card. When this is the case, hand him a copy of the Option Card that you keep at your desk or in your pocket. You may also want to put Option Card folders in the music room, art room, gym, resource room, library, nurse's office, and the substitute teacher folder. Be sure to inform other staff members that they may need to keep the Option Cards readily accessible so they can hand them to the student with AS as soon as they notice he needs one. Figure 3.8 shows examples of Option Cards.

I don't understand the directions.	*It is too loud in here.*
• I'll raise my hand and wait for the the teacher to come to me. • I will use my signal for help.	• I will go to my home base. • I will read a book at my desk.

Figure 3.8. Option cards.

When going to a restaurant, my son often needs an Option Card because the noise, crowded and busy atmosphere, and lack of familiarity result in heightened anxiety. I carry an Option Card for him that has the following choices: *Read your book or draw battleships in your sketch book* – two of his favorite activities. He enjoys these activities, they keep him focused on something other than the noise and crowd in the restaurant, and they provide a visual reminder of what he should do rather than a verbal reminder, which would be impossible for him to process once his anxiety level has risen.

Anxiety levels rise quickly in the person with AS. Be prepared. You may want to ask the student's parents to help you create Option

Cards. They will be able to tell you which situations trigger anxiety for the student and which situations may start her rage cycle. As the student becomes accustomed to the school environment and learns to deal with feelings of anxiety and sensory discomfort, you may need to change the options.

Job Cards

Job Cards may be used for classroom chores assigned on a rotational basis to all students as well as for specific jobs the student with AS is required to do regularly. Job Cards can be made using sentence strips or a rectangular piece of poster board with the numbers 1 to 4 and the word STOP written across the top (see Figure 3.9). The card is laminated and a small piece of Velcro™ is glued below each number. (Some children with AS have sensitive hearing and are aversive to the sound Velcro makes. If that is the case, pockets may be used to hold the word or picture cards rather than attaching them to the board with Velcro.) Write, draw, cut out pictures of each step involved in completing the job and attach Velcro to the back of each word or picture. The student attaches the picture cards or word cards to the chart in a sequence of four steps. The stop sign at the end of the card is the signal to the student that she has completed the job (see Figure 3.9).

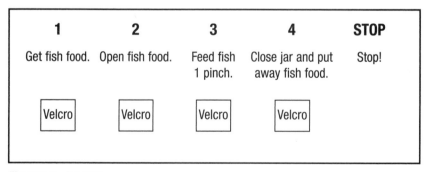

Figure 3.9. Job card.

Often students with AS have trouble recognizing when a job, activity, or task has been completed. This visual aid enables them to gain independence while working on sequencing skills, following directions, and self-direction (McClannahan & Krantz, 1999). Like all the other visual aids described in this chapter, Job Cards may be adapted to meet varying ability levels.

An excellent resource for creating and using visuals like Activity Plans and Job Cards is *Activity Schedules for Children with Autism: Teaching Independent Behavior* (McClannahan & Krantz, 1999). The authors explain methods for using activity schedules and the book includes photos of many of the visual aids presented.

The Power Card Strategy

Students with Asperger Syndrome are often difficult to motivate because they are withdrawn, disinterested in new or different experiences, or are engrossed in their own special interests (Gagnon, 2001). One of the best ways to motivate these children is to use the Power Card Strategy developed by Elisa Gagnon (2001). This highly effective visual is unique in that it makes use of the child's special interest as a motivating tool. Power Cards may be used to motivate students to practice social skills, do school work, or perform the steps in a routine such as those required to gather materials to take home at the end of the day.

The Power Card Strategy contains two components: a script and the Power Card. A teacher or parent develops a brief script written at the child's comprehension level detailing a problem situation or target behavior that includes a description of the behavior and describes how the child's special interest has addressed that social challenge. This solution is then generalized back to the child. The Power Card, the size of a business card or trading card, contains a picture of the special interest and a simply worded statement of behavioral expectations in two or three brief sentences.

In the case below, 8-year-old Kimberly's interest is dinosaurs so her teacher created a story about Darla the Dinosaur following the rules in music class and therefore setting an example for Kimberly.

Darla the Dinosaur goes to a school, just like you! She also goes to music class, just like you! Darla wants you to have as much fun as she does in music class so she wants you to remember to do the following:

1. Find your seat and sit down.

2. Keep your stress ball in your hands.

3. Do not touch other children.

Darla the Dinosaur is very proud of you when you remember to do these three things!

Figure 3.10. Sample power card.

Emergency Card

Emergencies such as a fire drill or a tornado warning can overwhelm and confuse students with AS. It is important to be prepared to help them during such a situation. Unprepared, students may exhibit behaviors you have never witnessed at school – they may hide, run away, scream, cry, and so on. The Emergency Card is an effective way to assist students to stay calm.

Use several large index cards to make the cards. Keep one at your desk, one at the student's desk, one by the door, and one with other staff members in the school. The rules on the card provide a visual reminder of what to do in an emergency situation and help the student to be cooperative. *Remember, when under stress or frightened, it is difficult for the person with AS to process auditory information.* A sample Emergency Card appears in Figure 3.11.

On the card, you can write the teacher's name so that the card would read, for example,

1. Stand next to Mrs. Walters.
2. Stay with Mrs. Walters.

Include a photo of the student standing next to the adult, so the student will be more likely to interpret the instructions when under stress.

```
┌─────────────────────────────────────────────┐
│               EMERGENCY CARD                 │
│                                              │
│   1. Stand next to _____ .  │
│                                              │
│   2. Stay with _____ .  │
│                                              │
└─────────────────────────────────────────────┘
```

Figure 3.11. Emergency card.

Older students may carry a business-card-sized Emergency Card with them at all times that includes the name of the homeroom teacher or resource teacher who could best handle the student if she were to become uncooperative. The following would be written on an Emergency Card for a student who carries his own card from class to class:

1. Tell the teacher you need to go to Mr. Billings' room.
2. Stay with Mr. Billings until he tells you to go back to your class.

For this example, the card would also include a picture of the student standing next to Mr. Billings.

Train the student to take out the Emergency Card and show it to an adult by rehearsing emergency situations and by scheduling unexpected practice drills. Repeated practice will help students who have difficulty remaining calm. Also inform staff members that the student with AS carries an Emergency Card so they can prompt him to use it when needed. Furthermore, be sure to give the staff a copy of the Emergency Card so they are familiar with the instructions on it and have a replacement card in the event the student with AS cannot find his own card.

Private Signals

If the student is uncomfortable asking for help, develop a hand signal or desk signal she can use in order to get the adult's attention discreetly. This can be anything from the student raising her hand with only the index finger extended to the student placing a brightly colored sticky note on her desk to get your attention. Be sure to include the student in determining what signal to use.

My son has an S.O.S. folder in which he keeps sheets of paper with the following written on it: "I have a problem. I need help with _____." All he has to do is write down his problem in the blank space. If he is too upset to write, he can take out the paper and just place it on his desk, signaling to the teacher that he needs help. The S.O.S. pages are yellow (we chose yellow because that color was not associated with any other subject), and his teacher and paraprofessionals know that if they see a yellow piece of paper on his desk, he needs help. When this happens, one of them goes to his desk, takes the paper, read its, and helps him without my son having to call attention to himself. When he is unable to write, his teachers discreetly ask him if he wants to talk about the problem in private. This is a great tool for helping children when they are having a problem and have difficulty asking for help.

Priming

Due to anxiety and difficulty generalizing, many students with AS engage in repetitive behaviors, meltdowns, or even shut down when they do not know what to expect at school. Priming (Wilde, Koegel & Koegel, 1992) is an effective way to prepare students for lessons and tests, make them aware of expectations, and familiarize them with routines. When priming, the primer presents class materials, schedules, expectations, and the like, the day before or the morning when the lesson, activity, or change is to occur. In some instances, priming may occur just prior to the activity.

Priming is an effective way to prepare students for lessons and tests . . .

Myles and Adreon (2001) recommend that the primer be someone who is patient and encouraging. Instead of using actual class materials, they also have been successful using lists or descriptions of activities to take place.

On several occasions, my son's teachers have sent home tests to be reviewed the night before a test so that he would know exactly what was expected of him. This simple accommodation greatly reduced his anxiety, making it possible for him to go to sleep the night before a test. Similarly, his teachers and paraprofessionals have presented teaching materials and schedules to him just prior to an activity or on the day before a schedule change. The time and effort they took to help familiarize him with the materials and schedule truly benefited him. Had this priming not taken place, more than likely he would have had difficulty focusing on schoolwork or maintaining composure. Priming is an extremely effective and relatively simple intervention for students with AS.

Assistive Technology

Assistive technology enables students with dysgraphia and processing problems, for example, to effectively communicate their ideas in writing while focusing on the content of their writing rather than on the physical act of writing. Tape recorders, writing tools such as *AlphaSmart, Co:Writer SmartApplet, Write:OutLoud,* and speech recognition software such as *Dragon Naturally Speaking* help students develop writing skills.

AlphaSmart

This is a small, portable word processor that is compatible with any computer. Many schools have these writing tools available for students with special needs. It is light weight and smaller than most laptop computers, so it is easy to carry by hand or in a backpack. Students who have used this tool say that they are able to complete their assignments more successfully because it is easier for them to type than to write with a pen or pencil. Another advantage of using an *AlphaSmart* is that it allows the student to read what she has written. That is, as text is typed, it appears on a small screen at the top of the keyboard so students do not have to try to decipher what they have written with a pencil on paper. This enables them to edit their own writing and take pride in their work. While students with AS may need direct instruction in keyboarding skills, often such training is more successful than working on improving handwriting skills.

Co:Writer

This is a software program that allows the student to use fewer keystrokes when typing by offering word choices as the student begins to type a word. For example, if the student types "I went to the p," the student can touch a function key to bring up word choices on the screen. Since the student ended with the letter *p*, the screen will display word choices that begin with *p*, such as *playground, park, pool, party.* Each word is displayed next to a number so that the student needs only to type a number to insert the word into her sentence. Beginning writers using the program may need to use the word choice function frequently, but as students develop keyboarding skills, they become less dependent on it and begin to type their own words. With this program, students are able to get more writing done than if they had to type every letter in a word, and it also helps them focus on putting thoughts and ideas into writing.

Co:Writer SmartApplet

This tool is an *AlphaSmart* that includes the *Co:Writer* program. Students who use this tool have a word prediction element available on their *AlphaSmart*, which allows them to type quickly and complete their work on time. When required to write by hand, Terrance writes a word or two and then stops, but when using the *Co:Writer SmartApplet,* he writes entire paragraphs. It is as if a key has unlocked the door to his ideas so he is able easily to record them in the *AlphaSmart*. Without this tool, Terrance's ingenious ideas stay locked away for only his mind to read.

Write:OutLoud

This easy-to-use talking word processing program reads each typed word aloud as the student types. This cross-platform software program has the capability to read aloud the entire written text as well as highlight text as it is read. Students who use this tool say that it helps them edit their papers because they can hear, as well as see, what they have written. *Write:OutLoud* also includes a homonym checker and a spell checker.

My son has used all three of these tools and they have enabled him to develop writing skills, independence, and self-confidence. Having improved his typing skills, he no longer needs the *Co:Writer* function or the *Write:OutLoud* program, but he continues to use the *AlphaSmart* daily, both at school and at home.

Dragon Naturally Speaking

This speech recognition software enables students to dictate their ideas rather than writing them. Thus, the program allows students to demonstrate their proficiency at written expression while freeing them from the physical act of writing. Students who are reluctant to write often produce longer and better papers when using this program than when they are required to write by hand. *Dragon Naturally Speaking* also enables students to work independently, as opposed to dictating their ideas to someone who writes for them. Some children with AS complain that the person doing the writing does not always write exactly what they say or tries to get them to change what they are saying. This program gives students a feeling of freedom as well as confidence to create their own ideas, important factors in developing writing skills.

Assistive technology helps students gain confidence in their writing ability.

Assistive technology helps students gain confidence in their writing ability and enables them to complete assignments.

Note-Taking Strategies

Note-taking can be confusing, difficult, and overwhelming to the student with AS. Typically, this skill is not taught at the elementary level. That is, note-taking skills are not taught like math or reading using direct teacher instruction with modeling, guidance, and practice. Nevertheless, once students enter third or fourth grade, most teachers expect them to be able to copy information from the chalkboard or projection screen without any instruction in how to do so.

Most third- or fourth-graders can do this. However, students with AS often find it difficult to copy information accurately, quickly, and neatly because of visual-motor difficulties, poor fine-motor skills, and tracking problems.

Main Ideas and Details

Similarly, taking notes from a text can seem an insurmountable task in the eyes of a student with AS. Because of over-selectivity and failure to attend to pertinent information, in addition to having tracking problems and poor fine-motor skills, they tend to copy information that is irrelevant or fail to complete the task. Frequently, students with AS are unable to identify the main ideas and details presented in a reading selection and, therefore, either write the material printed in the book almost word for word, or write only a word or two from a chapter. When this is the case, students need direct instruction in how to identify main ideas and details when reading.

In teaching this skill, the adult begins by asking the student to read aloud the first paragraph in the reading selection, or the student follows along as the adult reads the first paragraph aloud. Next, the adult asks the student, "What is important to remember from what we have just read?" The student may not know how to identify pertinent information, so the adult must tell her what is important, review the topic of the reading selection, and tell the student why this information needs to be included in the notes. This method works best in a quiet, 1:1 setting where the student can concentrate on learning how to identify important information from text.

In searching for alternatives to standard note-taking, it is important to explore a variety of techniques until you and the student find a technique that he is able to use successfully. Before you begin, however, make sure the student is able to identify main ideas and details in a given passage, as mentioned above. For some students with AS, this can be accomplished using the general education materials for teaching main idea and details provided in your reading program or by using the technique previously explained. Be aware that it may take several weeks or months to teach this skill because some students with AS need more time than neurotypical students. Therefore, set aside extra time by reducing the student's work load and arrange for a paraprofessional or teacher to work 1:1 with the student.

Once the student has learned how to identify main ideas and details, it is time to begin note-taking. The following note-taking strategies, which I have named the Coffee Breaks, offer students a break in having to do all the work that is usually expected in note-taking, and they also teach them how to take notes accurately and meaningfully. The strategies are presented in order of least to most amount of writing required. (Students may either write or dictate the information to be included in the notes.) As is the case for identifying main ideas and details, students with AS need direct, explicit instruction in how to use these strategies in frequent, short, 1:1 sessions. They can be taught by the teacher or a paraprofessional who has been instructed in how to use them. It is also beneficial to teach the strategies to parents of students with AS so the same strategies can be used at home.

Half & Half

When using this method, the student reads the material prior to the class lecture/presentation. To take notes on the reading material, the student uses loose-leaf paper or a spiral notebook and folds each piece of paper in half vertically. The left side of the page is entitled Book Notes and the right side of the page, Class Notes. After reading the material, the student writes his notes from the book on the left side of the page, leaving the right side blank, ready to fill in during the class lecture. Remember, the student must be able to identify main idea and details before he can use this method.

Colored pencils or markers can be used to write chapter subtitles or important vocabulary from the text. This helps keep the student organized during the note-taking process and makes the task of studying the notes easier because color facilitates visual processing of information. Many individuals with AS are visual thinkers, and it is much easier for them to locate vocabulary words or specific sections in a chapter to study when they know that vocabulary words are written in purple and the chapter subtitles are written in red. Table 3.8 presents an example of a reading selection from a social studies book followed by notes using the Half & Half strategy in Figure 3.12.

TABLE 3.8
Sample Reading Selection for Social Studies

AMERICAN SYMBOLS

A symbol is something that stands for something else. In America, we have three important symbols: the Liberty Bell, the American Flag, and the Statue of Liberty. In this chapter, you will read about these American symbols and what they represent to the American people.

The Liberty Bell

The Liberty Bell was placed in the capitol building in Philadelphia and rung for the first time in 1753. When it was placed there, America was still under the control of England. However, the American people wanted to be free from England. Americans declared themselves free from England in 1776, and the Liberty Bell was rung to call people to the capitol building to listen to the reading of the Declaration of Independence. The Liberty Bell has cracked twice and could not be repaired the second time. Even though the bell is cracked and cannot be rung anymore, it still reminds Americans of our freedom from England's rule.

The American Flag

When our country gained its freedom from England, there were only 13 states. That is why the American flag has 13 stripes. But did you know that the first American flag also had just 13 stars on the blue square? Each star represented one state, just like the red and white stripes. As our country grew and added more states, the flag changed. Our government decided to keep the original 13 stripes to represent the first 13 states in our nation, but they also decided to add one star on the blue square for every new state added to our nation. The American flag is displayed over every public building and school in our nation. It represents America and our belief in freedom for everyone in America.

The Statue of Liberty

The Statue of Liberty stands over New York harbor. In 1886, the people of France gave it to America, in honor of our 100th year of independence from England. It welcomes people who travel into New York harbor, standing tall above the water with the torch raised, showing the way to freedom. The Statue of Liberty is a symbol of freedom to all people who come to America.

BOOK NOTES	CLASS NOTES
Symbol – something that stands for something else – America has three symbols that represent freedom	**Symbol**
Liberty Bell – in Philadelphia – rung when Dec. of Independence was read in 1776 – cracked two times, not repaired – reminds Am. of freedom from England	**Liberty Bell**
American Flag – 1st flag had 13 stripes & 13 stars – now flag has 13 stripes and 50 stars: 1 stripe for each original state and 1 star for each state in U.S. – flag flies over all public bldgs. & schools in Am. – reminds people of freedom everywhere in Am.	**American Flag**
Statue of Liberty – given to Am. in 1886 (gift from France) – in NY harbor – symbol of freedom to people who come to Am.	**Statue of Liberty** Lazarus (poet): "Give me your tired"

Figure 3.12. Half & half notes.

The bold words in the notes in Figure 3.12 are the ones that should be written with a marker or colored pencil. By writing the chapter subtitles (i.e., Liberty Bell, American Flag, Statue of Liberty) in a color different from the rest of the notes, the student can readily locate information within his notes. This is important for study purposes as well as during the class lecture so he can quickly locate information being discussed. If everything were written in pencil or in blue ink, it would be difficult for the student with AS to locate and track information within the notes and keep up with the discussion/lecture.

During the class discussion of the chapter, the student adds any information to his notes that he has not already included. For example, if the teacher tells the class that the Statue of Liberty stands on a pedestal that is inscribed with the words "Give me your tired, your poor, your huddled masses yearning to breathe free" by the American poet Emma Lazarus, the student would add that information to her notes on the Class Notes side of the paper, directly opposite her book notes on the Statue of Liberty (see Figure 3.12). It is easy to locate the section in the notes on the Statue of Liberty since the words "Statue of Liberty" are written in a color. Using this strategy, the student with AS is able to keep up with the lesson and write down pertinent information from the teacher's lecture.

Cream & Sugar

Using this strategy, the teacher, paraprofessional, or volunteer serves as a guide while the student takes notes from a book, helping the student discern what is relevant. This method works well for assignments that require the student to do research and take notes from various resources. For instance, if the student is researching American symbols of freedom, she may need to be told what to include from a paragraph on the American flag, such as in Table 3.8. She will need to be told that the flag is a symbol of freedom along with an explanation of why. The adult assistant also helps the student write a brief statement about the American flag in her notes. Even though the student may have received direct instruction in identifying main idea and details, she may still require support when the actual task of note-taking is put before her.

Decaf

The Decaf method involves decreasing the amount of note-taking required. That is, the student reads the entire assignment, but only takes notes on a portion of it and is provided with notes on the rest. For example, if the assignment were the following: "Read Chapter 6 - The Three Branches of Government in the U.S. (pages 45-50) and take notes on the chapter," the student with AS might be assigned to take notes on just the section in the chapter that explains the judicial branch of government. Notes from the other sections in the chapter would be provided. As with all strategies for note-taking, support may be necessary to ensure that the student records relevant information in her notes.

If the student will be tested on the material, be sure to provide her with the rest of the notes, which can be written by the teacher, para-professional, or a volunteer. However, if the objective of the assignment is to practice note-taking skills, it is not necessary to give the student notes from the rest of the reading assignment. When using the Decaf method, the student feels less anxious about the assignment and performs well on a smaller task rather than poorly on a large task.

Instant

The Instant method consists of an outline on which the student fills in missing bits of information. After receiving a teacher-written outline of a chapter or a reading selection, the student reads the chapter to fill in the details that are missing from the outline. For example, chapter subtitles would already be included on the outline with details and examples from the section, except for one or two details that the student would fill in. The outline must follow the chapter exactly, with subtitles, examples, details, and vocabulary listed in the same order as they appear in the book. In this way, the student can follow along in the outline, adding missing bits of information as she reads each section in the chapter. This method helps keep the student focused as she progresses through the chapter and also underscores what is relevant. Finally, the completed outline can be used as a study guide for tests.

Student Presentations

A good approach to teaching children with AS is to start at the smallest and least complex level possible and then progress to the larger and more complicated levels. This pertains to both academic instruction and classroom environment. For example, some students with AS are not comfortable speaking in front of groups. Allow such students to speak in front of one other student at first. Then have them practice doing a presentation in front of two or three students until they are able to do it in front of the entire class.

Another approach used by Mrs. Napoli, an elementary teacher, was to allow her student with AS to whisper in her ear what he wanted to say to the class. The continued patience and reassurance this teacher offered the boy throughout the school year eventually enabled him to speak in front of the whole class. If Mrs. Napoli had not offered such support and understanding, this student may not have been able to represent his class the following

Some students with AS are not comfortable speaking in front of groups.

year on the student council. When he was nominated for classroom representative, his teachers, therapists, and parents were amazed and thrilled! The confidence that the boy gained at school will impact his life forever. I know that to be true because I am his mom!

The student with AS can acquire the skill to speak in front of a class, but it may take several months for her to gain the confidence to do so. Allow the student to observe classmates giving presentations before doing one herself. Be sure to give her a specific list of expectations, and provide several opportunities to practice prior to the formal presentation. If the student is very anxious, have her present just a portion or allow her to choose a partner to do the presentation with her. Some teachers help by standing next to the student and assisting during presentations. That way, the focus is not solely on the student, which gives her time to develop confidence and helps reduce anxiety.

Another strategy for teaching students how to give an oral presentation is to allow them to videotape the presentation in private and then show the recording to the class. Similarly, students can use overhead transparencies or visual display programs like PowerPoint™ to give a presentation. Again, this takes the focus off the student and provides an opportunity to share information while alleviating some of the pressure and nervousness students feel when giving a presentation face to face.

Using an Assignment Notebook

Assignment notebooks are extremely important for students with AS by helping them stay organized, keeping the parents informed of due dates and assignments, and serving as a means of teaching responsibility to students. While more elaborate systems are available, a three-ring, zippered binder that contains the assignment notebook and a take-home pocket folder works well. This system can be used in the primary grades and continued into junior and senior high schools. To get the most benefit out of using the assignment notebook, make sure the student follows a routine for recording homework assignments, and make certain that the notebook is checked daily by both teachers and parents.

As illustrated in Figure 3.13, when the student is completing her assignment notebook, it is recommended that she also record the approximate time to be spent on a given assignment or activity. Many students with AS have difficulty comprehending and managing the concept of time and often get lost in the details, spending two hours on an assignment that should take 20 minutes to complete.

Some students with AS have difficulty getting all of the details written down in the assignment notebook because of time constraints, poor fine-motor skills, and/or tracking problems. My son has struggled with this every year in elementary school. To accommodate him, his teachers have used the following strategies:

1. Have a paraprofessional fill in the assignments for him.
2. Provide white stickers with typical assignments written on individual stickers. (For example, he had stickers that said *Spelling W/S, Math W/S, Soc. Studies: read pgs.,* and *Reading: read pgs.* When he had a spelling worksheet to complete for homework, he would put the *Spelling W/S* sticker on the assignment notebook page, thus eliminating the need to write it all down, but still requiring him to take responsibility for recording it in his notebook. Similarly, when he had a reading assignment for social studies or reading group, he simply placed the corresponding sticker in his assignment notebook and wrote the page numbers of the assignment down.)

Homework for _____

Subject	Assignment	Due Date	Priority	Time to Complete	Done
Math					
Reading					
Spelling					
Social Studies					
Add Subject					

_____
Parent's Signature

Comments: _____
_____
_____
_____

_____
Teacher's Signature

Comments: _____
_____
_____
_____

_____
Other (paraprofessional, inclusion
facilitator, SLP, OT)

Comments: _____
_____
_____
_____

Figure 3.13. Sample page from an assignment notebook.

3. Allow him to arrive early, before other children, so he can record the assignments in his notebook without the distractions of noise and moving children and without the stress of time constraints. (This strategy worked very well, and as his anxiety level was reduced, he felt more relaxed and was able to concentrate on accomplishing the task!)

4. Give him a copy of a completed assignment notebook page to copy so he does not have to copy the information from the chalkboard or rely on auditory memory when the assignment is presented verbally.

Check the assignment notebook before the student leaves school to make sure everything has been recorded properly. This step is as important as having the student fill in the assignments. If he has not recorded things accurately, he may be confused when trying to complete assignments, and parents may be confused or help with the wrong assignment – all of which may result in tantrums, rage, and meltdowns. When this occurs, it is impossible to get the child back on track. And as a result, he may fail to complete homework, find the process impossible, and refuse to try future assignments. Therefore, check the notebook daily to see that everything is recorded accurately!

Check the notebook daily to see that everything is recorded accurately!

After the assignment notebook has been checked by the teacher, the student can take it home, show it to a parent before beginning assignments, and have a parent sign it when he is finished doing homework. The assignment notebook may be signed by the parents even when little or no homework has been completed, and this should be acceptable. Many children with AS are often so stressed from the school day with all of the social, sensory, and physical demands it places on them that they are incapable of focusing on school work once they get home. Be accepting of children with AS who need a reduction in the number of homework assignments and/or need to be exempt from completing assignments. Encourage parents to sign the notebook every day, even when their child is unable to complete assignments. Having open lines of communication between parents and teachers benefits the student greatly. When everyone is aware of what the student with AS can and cannot tolerate or accomplish, more appropriate expectations will be placed on him, enabling him to find success at school.

When the student is not able to complete an assignment, the parent should write a brief message to the teacher explaining the reason. At times, my son was unable to do his homework, either because he was too stressed from the school day or because he had after-school activities such as violin lessons, Tae Kwon Do, or occupational therapy – all important for improving his motor skills and sensory processing. In those instances, I wrote a note in the assignment notebook explaining why he was unable to complete the assignments. For example, when he was too stressed or anxious, I wrote, "Difficult day." I did not have to go into great detail because the teacher and I had discussed this at the beginning of the school year and she automatically knew this meant that he was nearing a TRM. When my son had many after-school activities, I wrote, "TKD and OT," and she knew he was only capable of getting through his martial arts class and therapy that day. This simple accommodation made life at home with my son much more relaxed and made me feel comfortable with the decision to reduce or omit homework assignments on days when it would have been difficult or impossible for him to do them. This is not to imply that he was always exempt from homework, but to demonstrate how parents and teachers can work together to determine what is appropriate for a given student.

After the assignment notebook has been signed, the student brings it back to school the following day and shows it to the teacher or paraprofessional. While this places monitoring responsibility on the parents, teachers and paraprofessionals, it is important for children with AS to have a support system. Left on their own to complete assignments and keep track of work, they usually are not successful – papers get lost, letters to the teacher are crumbled up, and homework is forgotten. Provide positive reinforcement for use of the assignment notebook and all efforts toward taking responsibility for homework.

Over time, the need for support is reduced as the student gains more independence and becomes familiar with the routine. This may take a few months or it may take a few years. Due to the importance of this organizational accommodation, it is important to coordinate the effort of supporting the student. Hold a team meeting that includes all of the student's teachers, his parents, and the student himself to discuss the use of the assignment notebook, the monitoring system, and the expectations of the student.

Homework

Depending on the degree of impairment, flexibility training (see Chapter Five), and home support, some students with AS are capable of completing homework, but modifications may be needed in the number or length of the assignments due to fine-motor difficulties and anxiety problems. When the homework assignment is to practice material the student has already mastered, consider excusing the student from doing the assignment.

During the school day, students with AS are bombarded with intense sensory input that can be very fatiguing. In addition, they can become stressed from all the fine-motor work and social interaction that is required throughout the day. Not surprisingly, these students are often exhausted, frustrated, and anxious by the time they get home. Many need to be in a quiet, stimulus-free environment to relax after the stresses of their day. Some need to engage in a favorite activity before they are ready to do any additional work. When a homework routine has been established that incorporates the student's relaxation time prior to doing the work, the student can better complete some assignments. Ask the parents to help you gauge the appropriate amount of homework for a given student. Table 3.9 is a homework plan we used for my son in elementary school.

TABLE 3.9
Home Work Plan

Grade	Time	Frequency
1	5-10 min.	2 or 3 days per week
2	10 min.	3 or 4 days per week
3	10-15 min.	3 or 4 days per week
4	15-20 min.	3 or 4 days per week

The time allotments listed above were maximum amounts we considered when creating his homework routine. This plan worked well for my son, but consider individual abilities and needs when creating a homework plan for other students with AS.

Teachers should develop a homework routine prior to the first day of school, whenever possible, so a pattern is established from the start. In the primary grades, homework for specific content areas can be given for each day of the week. Table 3.10 shows sample homework routines.

TABLE 3.10
Sample Homework Routines

Day	Homework Assignment
Monday	Spelling Worksheet
Tuesday	Math Activity
Wednesday	Reading
Thursday	Social Studies

In the upper grades, homework and tests can be given on specific days of the week. For example:

Day	Homework Assignment	Test
Monday	Spelling & Reading	Spelling Pretest
Tuesday	Math & Social Studies	Reading Test
Wednesday	Math & Reading	Social Studies Test
Thursday	Spelling & Reading	Math Test
Friday		Spelling Posttest

When this method is used, the student does not have to study for several tests that all occur on the same day. Reading tests may not be given every Tuesday and math tests may not be given every Thursday, but the student knows what to expect, making her less likely to become anxious about homework and test preparation. As the student learns the schedule and begins to use the assignment notebook independently, she is able to take responsibility for homework assignments. When the homework is predictable and the assignments are manageable, parental and teacher involvement with homework help can eventually be decreased.

Organizational accommodations, as discussed in this chapter, create structure and predictability for students with AS. Once these accommodations are in place, it is easier to modify learning objectives and develop strategies to more effectively teach specific concepts and skills.

> *Organizational accommodations create structure and predictability.*

Assessments

Students with AS need direct instruction and practice in every form of assessment they will be given, and at times they will need an alternative form of testing. Teach them how to take tests by providing a practice test that includes questions similar to those on the actual test and allowing time to review the material privately with the teacher.

Allow students who have writing problems due to dysgraphia to use assistive technology and/or give verbal answers. Likewise, tests can be shortened or additional time can be given to accommodate for dysgraphic problems, in addition to providing paper with wide spaces and lines for writing answers.

True-False Tests

These are difficult for many students with AS because statements can be false for a number of reasons: One word is incorrect, multiple words are incorrect, and the meaning is implied as opposed to being directly stated. In addition, words like *some* or *many* may lead to confusion or the student may spend too much time interpreting individual statements. For example, students may have difficulty with the following true-false statement because they attend to unimportant information:

Some mammals live on land.

Students with AS may consider this answer false because they do not see it as *absolutely true*, reading this to say that *some* mammals live on land is not the same as *many* mammals live on land. In this instance, the student has attended to information in the statement that is irrelevant, rather than to the intended qualifier – *land*. This is a common error among students with AS, so be sure to interpret true-false test results with caution, or better, offer some question/answer choices in another format such as multiple choice.

Multiple-Choice Tests

These are one of the best test options for students with AS because they require little writing. However, two problems may arise when using this type of test:

- Students may have trouble writing the correct answer choice in the correct space when they have to write letters or numbers that correspond to an answer.
- Students may not be able to keep track of which answers they have used.

Therefore, check the student's answer sheet to make sure he is recording answers properly and crossing out choices that have already been selected.

Fill-in-the-Blank Tests

These are also good choices for students with AS. When using this type of test, it is best to offer a word bank that contains the answers needed to fill in the blanks. In doing so, the student is provided with visual cues to help with recall. (Remember, students with AS are visual thinkers.) The word bank is also important because it limits the number of choices, preventing students from spending too much time trying to discover ALL of the possibilities for filling the blank. My son finds fill-in-the-blank tests amusing, trying to find as many words or phrases as possible to put in the blanks. He does not typically write them down, but he spends test time pondering the possibilities and then recites the test questions and his funny answers to me when he arrives home.

Wording

Make sure questions are clearly worded. Students with AS can become anxious during tests, making comprehension difficult. For those who have difficulty comprehending what they read, accurate wording becomes even more important. For example, on essay tests where students read a prompt and then recall information, make comparisons, and the like, check to make sure the student understands what he is required to do. Also, because students with AS often focus on details rather than the main idea, they may not attend to the important information in the question and answer it incorrectly even when they know the correct answer. For example, my son incorrectly answered this test question:

*"How have natural and man-made changes
affected the Southeast region of the U.S.?"*

Even though social studies is his favorite subject and he knew all of the test material prior to the test, his response did not reflect this. He misinterpreted the language in the question and dictated the following:

*"There are various bodies of water like
rivers, lakes, and the Atlantic Ocean."*

Clearly, he did not understand the question. If it had been restated, more than likely he would have answered it correctly. My son's speaking vocabulary is large and at times he astounds adults who hear him talk. But frequently his reading comprehension difficulties prohibit him from interpreting written language accurately. His paraprofessionals are aware of this now and offer him assistance when they notice that he is having difficulty interpreting test questions.

As seen in the example above, some students may need the question restated in simpler terms, some may need the question rewritten, and some may need explanations of terms and phrases used in a question. This is true for all types of assessments, so be prepared to modify test questions. In addition, when teachers or paraprofessionals read test directions to students with AS, they make the task of test-taking much less stressful for them because that allows them to ask questions as soon as they are confused.

Seeking Clarification

Allow the student to ask questions during the test. Often students with AS are just looking for reassurance while they are taking tests, not for clues about the answers. (They have trouble reading faces so they will NOT be looking for clues to the right answers in your expressions!) When using this option, you may want to limit the number of questions, and be sure to tell the student ahead of time how many questions he will be permitted to ask.

As a means of preparing for tests, give the student with AS an outline on which she fills in missing information or give her teacher-written notes. Some teachers ask other students in the class to share their notes. If teachers choose to do this, they must check the notes for clarity and accuracy before giving them to the student with AS. In addition to giving the student an outline or notes, review the material prior to the test to ascertain that she has a good understanding of the test material.

Fatigue

Some students with AS become fatigued during the school day because of poor motor skills, hypotonia, and/or sensory overload. When this happens, they may shut down, finding the task of test-taking impossible. In such cases, consider an alternative time and/or location for the student to complete the test so he has an opportunity to complete it when and where he is capable of working up to his potential. Alternative locations include the resource room, a private office, a quiet board or meeting room in the school, a study carrel, or the library. Do not put a desk in a closet as this has a negative impact on a student with AS, making him feel either punished or confined to an undesirable location.

Other ways to help students with AS during tests include offering a physical activity or sensory break, and asking the student if he wants you to read the test to him. Doing something physical like taking a walk or squeezing some Play-Doh™ for a brief period of time often helps reduce anxiety in the student with AS. My son kept a sensory box at the back of his classroom when he was a second- and third-grader. The box contained a small plastic container of uncooked rice, some Play-Doh, a Koosh™ ball, and bubble wrap. When he became anxious or fatigued during tests, he was permitted to take his box to his desk or to a table at the back of the room and fidget with the items in the box until he felt better. This usually took about 10 minutes, after which he would be prompted with a hand signal or verbal reminder to return the box to the shelf where it was stored. Another boy with AS takes messages to the office when he is having difficulty sitting through an entire test. This little break helps him refocus and perform better. These simple accommodations can help students with AS perform up to their potential on tests.

You may also allow the student to take the test in a quiet area if he is not able to concentrate in the classroom since many students with AS have very sensitive hearing and even the slightest noise in the class or from the hallway may be distracting.

Test-Taking Skills

Teach test-taking skills by practicing different types of questions and recording answers. This reduces test-anxiety and helps the student remember what to do in a variety of test situations. Students with AS benefit from direct instruction and practice in test-taking skills including:

Students with AS benefit from direct instruction and practice in test-taking skills.

- Using an answer sheet
- Interpreting a graph, picture, and diagram
- Identifying similarities and differences
- Determining relationships/associations

- Recognizing faulty or erroneous information
- Sequencing information
- Determining cause and effect
- Recalling information
- Generalizing/applying information
- Analyzing information
- Evaluating information

If materials are not available at school to teach these skills, teachers can use resources such as *Basic Skills Series: Test-Taking Skills,* published by Instructional Fair, and *Test-Taking Skills,* published by Frank Schaffer Publications. Both of these resources are available for grade levels 1 through 6. Each grade-level book contains reproducible student activity materials, test-taking tips, and answer keys, making them easy to use for the teacher and student.

In addition to practicing test-taking skills, students with AS also benefit from practicing different types of tests such as matching, cloze, multiple-choice, true-false, fill-in-the-blank, and short answer. Practice should begin as early in the student's schooling as possible. Introduce test-taking practice in first grade, if possible, and always start at the beginning of the school year. This alleviates anxiety and provides students with the opportunity to learn about tests in a manner that is effective for them – actual practice and rehearsal. Since they typically have trouble generalizing from real-life situations, they do not acquire test-taking skills and knowledge about tests the way most neurotypical students do. That is, they do not learn what to expect on tests and how to answer test questions just by being placed in test-taking situations. To be successful at test-taking, most students with AS need direct, 1:1 teacher-guided practice in how to take tests, as recommended in this section.

Because of their high anxiety levels and impulsiveness, students with AS do not always perform up to their potential on tests. They may do well in class and on homework assignments, but poorly on tests. If test scores are not indicative of their actual mastery or knowledge of a concept, consider alternative means of assessment such as verbal rather than written responses and providing

Because of their high anxiety levels and impulsiveness, students with AS do not always perform up to their potential on tests.

assistance during the exam to help with the anxiety and to keep the student from responding impulsively. Other modifications include allowing the student to tape record answers or use drawing and diagramming.

Caring teachers can have an incredible impact on the lives of their students. Given the right environment, strategies, and encouragement, children can accomplish amazing tasks. Give them the opportunity and time they need to grow and learn to adjust to school. It *WILL* make a difference.

CHAPTER FOUR

Accommodations in the Curriculum

In addition to organizational accommodations such as those discussed in Chapter Three, many students with AS need modifications in the way curriculum is presented and in the way they are required to complete and present their school work. In general, complex instructions are difficult for them to understand, so when giving instructions, teachers need to:

- simplify instructions by reducing the number of steps or words
- repeat complex directions
- check for understanding when directions are given verbally
- put directions in writing, whenever possible

This chapter offers effective ways to modify the elementary school curriculum for students with AS. By following these suggestions, in combination with the organizational accommodations presented in the previous chapter, educators will greatly increase the chances of successful performance of students with AS.

Math

Some students with AS have difficulty learning math or demonstrating mastery of math skills and concepts due to dysgraphia, poor eye-hand coordination, inferencing problems, impulsivity, anxiety, and memory retrieval problems. (Please note: Some students with AS are superior mathematicians, capable of performing well above grade level in spite of any impairments due to AS.) For students who experience difficulties in math, the following strategies will provide a means to success.

Organizational Strategies

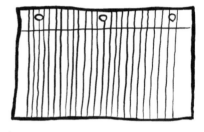

Rather than having the student write out math problems on lined paper in the usual manner where the lines run horizontally, turn the paper sideways and allow the student to utilize the columns created by the lines.

In this way, the columns serve to keep the numbers properly aligned and facilitate independence as the student learns to keep track of place value by using the columns. Graph paper can be used in the same way by having the student use the rows and columns of boxes to keep numbers and problems aligned properly.

Have the student use colored pencils with erasers (for easy correcting) for each step in a mathematical algorithm. For example, when completing a multiplication problem that requires multiplying a three-digit number by a two-digit number, different-colored pencils may be used for each step of the process. When combined with the strategy of turning the paper sideways as suggested above, the student finds the process much easier and gains confidence and proficiency more quickly than when doing the work in the traditional manner.

Worksheets can be overwhelming when there are many problems on the page. To avoid this problem, cut the page into sections and give the student one section at a time or enlarge the print and copy on to several pages. In this way, the student is better able to stay on task and complete the work.

Manipulatives

As emphasized throughout this book, children with AS are visual thinkers. This means that when they are thinking about something, they see images in their mind like a VCR replaying a scene (Grandin, 1995). If you use manipulatives to teach skills and concepts, you enable students to form a visual reference in their minds to be used as needed. Before teaching a student how to perform a particular type of math skill, show him what the skill or concept means in visual terms. Base 10 Blocks™, beans, beads, and Unifix™ cubes are examples of manipulatives appropriate for elementary students. Use these manipulatives to teach concepts such as place value and trading/borrowing as well as algorithms such as adding, subtracting, multiplying, and dividing.

When teaching subtraction, for example, Unifix cubes help demonstrate what is involved in the process. For the problem $8 - 3 = ?$, put together a column of five red cubes with three blue cubes. Have the student count the total number of red and blue cubes in the column (8) and then take off the three blue ones to arrive at the correct answer: five red cubes. The use of color and hands-on manipulation of the cubes enables the student to visually process the steps in solving subtraction problems.

Some children with AS have trouble mastering basic math facts but can process higher-level concepts with great facility. Often the basic facts are taught verbally, which means students must use their auditory memories to access the information. This is a major challenge for students with AS, who typically are not auditory but visual and kinesthetic learners. For the student who experiences difficulty mastering basic facts, math manipulatives provide a visual and tactile means of learning the facts.

Other students with AS are able to master basic facts because of their prodigious rote memories, yet find problem-solving and multiple-step processes troublesome. For the student who has difficulty solving multiple-step problems such as $(2 \times 4) - 3$, Base 10 Blocks can be used to break the problem into manageable steps. Begin by showing the student how to calculate 2×4 with the blocks. Next, show her that she must take away 3 blocks from the group of 8 blocks (the product of 2×4). This method demonstrates the process involved in multiple-step problems with countable, moveable blocks, thus locking the process into the student's memory because the teaching method consists of both visual and kinesthetic components.

Word Problems

Word or story problems are difficult for students with AS who have language and cognitive difficulties. For example, the wording may be confusing such as in the following story problem:

> *Jodi baked 18 cookies and 12 brownies.*
> *How many more cookies did she bake?*

The student with AS may have trouble with this problem because it does not say specifically what must be compared to the cookies in order to solve the problem. Most third-graders who have the ability to make inferences are able to solve this problem because they can deduce that the number of cookies is being compared to the number of brownies, but students with AS often lack the ability to infer from either written or spoken language.

Another example of a type of word problem that poses difficulty for students with AS is the following:

> *The average wind speed in San Diego is 17 km/h.*
>
> *The highest wind speed in San Diego was*
> *11 km/h faster than 6 times the average.*
> *What was the highest wind speed?*

This problem requires the student to decipher what is meant by *11km/h faster than 6 times the average* before she can attempt to solve it. The student may be confused because she has to translate words into algorithms while sequencing the order of operations in order to determine the correct answer. That is, she must determine that *11 km/h faster* means to add and that she must add 11 after she has calculated the value of 6 times 17. The complexity of the math problem, combined with the complexity of the language used in the problem, makes it difficult to solve.

Some student with AS may attend to insignificant information such as in this problem:

The store had only 24 baseballs left.
Carl bought 7 of them.
What fraction of the baseballs did he buy?

When attempting to solve this problem, a student with AS replied, "I cannot figure this out because the problem does not tell me how many baseballs there were at first, only how many were *left.*" Another student with AS said that there are 17 baseballs left. When asked how she came to that conclusion, she answered that she saw the word *left* and knew that *left* is a clue to subtract, so she subtracted 7 from 24 to get 17.

When the goal is for the student to master mathematical operations rather than decipher complex written language, which is often included in a word problem, you may want to rewrite the problems to ensure the language is not confusing. For example, the cookie problem can be rewritten like this:

Jodi baked 18 cookies and 12 brownies.
How many more cookies did she bake than brownies?

With this simple change, the student now knows to compare cookies to brownies and is able to solve the problem. Similarly, the baseball problem can be rewritten like this:

The store had 24 baseballs. Carl bought 7 of them.
What fraction of the baseballs did Carl buy?

Notice that the words *only* and *left* were omitted and the pronoun *he* was changed to *Carl* because pronouns are confusing to some individuals with AS. With these simple changes, it was easier for the student to understand the problem.

Types of problems

Once the student can read the problem, it is time to teach her how to identify what type of problem it is. The types of word problems that elementary students typically encounter are included in Table 4.1.

Identifying the type of problem presented helps the student choose the algorithm or steps needed to solve it. The cookie problem above is a comparison problem, so the student needs to subtract in

TABLE 4.1
Types of Word Problems

- Find the total (add or multiply)
- What's the difference (subtract)
- Make a comparison (subtract)
- Find a pattern (+,-, x, / by the same number)
- How many combinations (multiply totals)
- How far (add or multiply)
- Find the missing number (multiply, then divide)
- How many containers (divide)
- Find the average (add, then divide)

order to solve it. After the student knows which algorithm to use, it is time to choose a strategy. Teach the student to use strategies such as drawing a picture or making a chart to help him gain proficiency at this type of work. The strategies presented in Table 4.2 can be taught to students in any grade in elementary school.

TABLE 4.2
Word-Problem Strategies

- Draw a picture (simple +,-, x, ÷, time of day)
- Make a chart (multiple categories and items/category)
- Use a table (finding/using a pattern)
- Use a number line (+,x, temperature, measurement)

Strategies

The strategy *Draw a Picture* can be used to solve the cookie problem. For example, the problem states that there are 18 cookies and 12 brownies, so the student should draw a picture of them: 18 circles and 12 squares to represent 18 cookies and 12 brownies. Using the picture, the student can now compare the number of cookies to the number of brownies by crossing off one circle for each square crossed off. Finally, the student can count the number of circles left and determine that there are 6 circles (or cookies) left.

The *Make a Chart* strategy is appropriate for word problems with multiple categories and several items in each category, such as in the following:

> *Coco the Clown has many outfits. Each day, he*
> *chooses a shirt, a pair of pants, and shoes. Coco has*
> *a red pair of pants and a blue pair. He has three shirts –*
> *one is red, another one is white with blue polka dots,*
> *and the last one is green. Coco also has a red pair*
> *of shoes and a yellow pair. How many different*
> *outfits can Coco make using these items?*

Figure 4.3 provides an example of how to solve this problem using a chart.

Problem-Solving Strategy: Make a Chart

Step 1:

pants	shirts	shoes
red	red	red
blue	white with polka dots	yellow
	green	
2	3	2

Step 2:

Pants: 2   shirts: 3   shoes: 2

Step 3:

2 x 3 = 6

Step 4:

6 x 2 = 12 outfits

Figure 4.3. Problem-solving strategy: Make a chart.

In solving this problem, the student creates a chart with three columns, one for each article of clothing (pants, shirts, shoes) and then lists each article of clothing under the appropriate category (Step 1). Next, he writes the total number of items in each category under each category (Step 2). He then multiplies the total number of items in the first category with the total number of items in the second category (Step 3), and multiplies that answer with the total number of items in the third category to arrive at the answer: 12 outfits (Step 4). This method for solving problems that requires determining a total number of combinations when there are several categories and items per category is much easier than having to list each item and draw lines back and forth across the page to match up items and then count the lines.

When the word problem requires finding a pattern such as in the problem below, teach the student to use a table (see Figure 4.4).

> *On the first day of counting tomatoes, John counted 4. Each day his tomato plant grew the same number of new tomatoes. On the fifth day of counting tomatoes, he had 12 tomatoes. How many new tomatoes grew each day? (Hint: find a pattern.)*

Day 1	Day 2	Day 3	Day 4	Day 5
4 + 2 =	6 + 2 =	8 + 2 =	10 + 2 =	12

Figure 4.4. Problem-solving stratey: Use a table.

To solve this problem use a table with only two rows to keep the problem visually simple and easy to decipher. In the top row, write the days (1-5). Then write the start number 4, directly below Day 1. Directly below Day 5, write 12. As you are doing these steps, explain them to the student. Hearing the steps repeated and seeing them done simultaneously helps lock them in the student's memory. Use short, simple statements. For example, say, "I know the start number is 4, so I write that under Day 1. I know the end number is 12, so I write that under Day 5." The student's job is to discover the pattern rule. For this problem, it is to add 2. Remember, students with AS often have difficulty comprehending word problems so you may have to provide assistance until they have gained proficiency at solving this type of problem. Help them along each step of the problem, narrating with simple sentences and giving assistance when they are unable to complete a step independently.

Number lines can also be very helpful when solving word problems, especially those involving temperature differences or changes. For example, a number line can be used to solve this problem:

> *The average temperature in Dallas for the month*
> *of May is 75 degrees. The average temperature*
> *in Dallas for the month of August is 21 degrees*
> *higher. What is the average temperature in Dallas*
> *for the month of August?*

To solve the problem above, the student starts at 75 and counts up 21 units on the number line to find the answer: 96 degrees. This method works well for students who have not yet mastered the algorithms for addition or subtraction. In working toward real-life application of mathematics, use a variety of number lines such as a ruler, tape measure, thermometer, yard or meter stick, or measuring cups with increments of measure written on them.

Another strategy to help students with AS solve word problems is to use a checklist, as illustrated in Table 4.3.

TABLE 4.3
Word Problem Checklist

_____ 1. Read the Problem

_____ 2. Identify the Type of Problem

_____ 3. Choose a Strategy

_____ 4. Solve the Problem

_____ 5. Check Your Answer

The checklist helps the student follow all the steps necessary for solving word problems, making them less stressful.

Repeated practice, systematic methods, and patient modeling help students with AS learn how to problem solve.

Tests

Math tests that are organized in a simple, straightforward manner on a page work best for students with AS. As suggested for math worksheets, provide the test material in large print with fewer items per page for students who have difficulty reading pages that contain a lot of information. Figure 4.5 illustrates a page of a math test that has been modified for a fourth-grade student with AS. The original test consisted of 20 problems presented on one page. The modified version consists of four pages, with five problems per page.

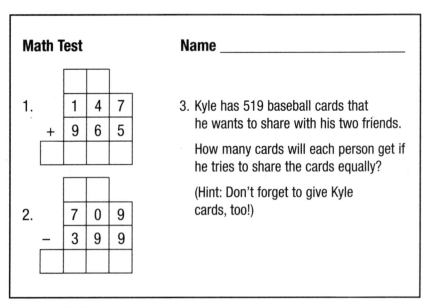

Figure 4.5. Modified math test.

Anxiety may interfere with the student's ability to complete a math test. Some students with AS worry about answering the problems correctly and end up spending too much time solving a particular problem. When this happens, they become anxious about not having enough time to finish the test and, as a result, often fail to complete it. With adult intervention, the student can learn to pace herself and complete the test on time. A simple nod or a check written next to a problem will cue the student to move on to the next problem. This is not to give the student feedback on the accuracy of her answers, but to keep her moving through the test. Offer positive reinforcements like stickers or points to students who have trouble in this area.

> *Anxiety may interfere with the student's ability to complete a math test.*

Another way to provide assistance during a test is to stop the student after every three or four problems to make sure she is recording the answers correctly. Some students with AS rush through their work, solving problems successfully but recording answers in the wrong space or copying them incorrectly.

As mentioned, when attempting to solve word problems, some students with AS have difficulty understanding the wording. Therefore, teachers or paraprofessionals may want to stop the students during the test and ask them to explain the problem. By doing so, you will know if they understand it or if they need it rewritten in language they can understand.

Other ways to help students with AS during tests include offering a physical activity break or a sensory break, or asking the student if she wants you to read the test to her. Some students become fatigued because of poor motor skills, hypotonia, and/or sensory overload. When this happens, they my shut down, finding the task of test-taking impossible. Consider an alternative time or location for the student to complete the test so that she may have an opportunity to complete it when she is capable of working up to her potential.

Using Special Interests

Many students with AS learn concepts better if they are connected to their personal interests, and perform well when permitted to demonstrate knowledge using means other than paper-and-pencil assessment. One of my son's special interests is maritime history, and we have used this interest to help teach him math skills and concepts. For example, he has practiced subtraction and word problems by solving problems related to ocean depth, ship size, longitude/latitude, distance, and passage of time. He has built models, made maps, and even drawn pictures to accompany word problems he has created, all relating to maritime history.

> *Many students with AS learn concepts better if they are connected to their personal interests.*

Math can be troublesome for students with AS. But using a variety of accommodations, such as reorganizing printed materials, utilizing colored pencils and markers, incorporating manipulatives, rewriting word problems, teaching problem-solving strategies, providing assistance with test-taking, and bringing in the students' special interest to motivate and reinforce teaching helps these students acquire math skills and develop an understanding of math concepts.

Writing

Writing can be difficult for students with AS for a variety of reasons. First, many have poor fine-motor skills, making the physical act of writing nearly impossible. Next, they have difficulty organizing their thoughts, transferring them from visual references into written language and presenting them in such a way that others understand what they wrote. Finally, many have trouble deciphering what is expected in the writing assignment because often it is presented verbally by the teacher or covers a topic that is derived from generalizing or analyzing past experience or previously read material – a task that is extremely difficult for students with AS.

In this section we will discuss handwriting, the writing process, organizational tools, and writing a first draft.

Handwriting

The physical task of writing is difficult for many students with AS because of frequent problems with fine-motor coordination. There are many ways to deal with this. Some teachers allow the students to print rather than use cursive, or vice versa, depending on which type of writing is easier for them. Others reduce the emphasis on neat handwriting. Yet others allow the student to dictate her thoughts to someone who serves as a secretary or scribe. If the student's motor skills improve, she can do some of her own writing, but some children with AS never become proficient with a pen or pencil, despite occupational therapy or other attempts to improve fine-motor skills such as squeezing clay, tracing lines and letters, or digging in sand. For these students, consider alternate means of recording their ideas.

The most valid way of obtaining and assessing the student's actual knowledge of a particular subject or proficiency in written expression may be to have someone like a paraprofessional or adult volunteer write down her story, answers on exams, or essay. As mentioned in Chapter Three, assistive technology is another means of accommodating the student who has problems with handwriting. Programs such as *AlphaSmart* and *Co:Writer* can provide much-needed assistance. In addition, teachers may consider permitting the student to use a computer, typewriter, or tape recorder to complete assignments.

The Writing Process

Individuals with AS may have difficulty formulating thoughts spontaneously and/or accessing experiential memories, which can negatively affect their ability to write from an unfamiliar prompt. Because of their neurological impairments, they retrieve information differently than the general population. As a result, a word or a sentence may not be a sufficient prompt for them to begin writing.

As a first-grader, Marianna was unable to write in her Monday journal, which caused a great deal of frustration for both Marianna and her teacher. Every Monday morning, Marianna's teacher wrote a prompt on the chalkboard and read it to the children. One morning she wrote *What did you do over the weekend?* As the children in the class began writing about their weekend or drawing pictures of what they had done, Marianna sat at her desk chewing on her pencil and ripping her paper. Before Marianna's teacher was aware of AS, she would send notes home to Marianna's mother, telling her how disappointed she was that Marianna wasted time during journal writing and that she thought Marianna was defiant. Indeed, Marianna was reluctant to write, but it was not out of defiance or laziness. She was unable to recall the details of her weekend the way the neurotypical children did. The written prompt on the chalkboard was not sufficient to trigger her memory. After learning about Marianna's diagnosis of AS, her parents suggested that the teacher try using visual prompts and a longer prewriting period to help Marianna with her writing. Fortunately for Marianna, her teacher took time to learn how to accommodate a student with AS and reported to the parents that the visual prompts and extra preparation time were successful in helping Marianna recall events. As a result, Marianna was able to draw pictures and write short sentences about her weekend experiences, holidays, friends, pets, and so on.

In order to write from a prompt, the student with AS will need extra preparation. Think of her mind as a computer. She will need adequate *search criteria* in order to access her ideas and memories. Teachers may find that the student is an expert on a particular topic and can deliver sentence after sentence of information pertaining to this topic. However, the same student may not be able to recall the events of her most recent birthday party. The best way to assist the student who has difficulty retrieving memories or forming ideas for writing is to plan for an extensive prewriting time. Visuals will help, so ask the student to bring pictures or other relevant items to aid in recalling her memories. In Marianna's case, the teacher would send a note home to her parents a week before a writing assignment would be given to let them know about it. This gave Marianna's mother time to gather pictures and other items to discuss with Marianna prior to the writing assignment. This extra preparation helped Marianna meet the narrative writing objective for her grade level.

In addition to parents working with a child prior to writing, a paraprofessional, peer, or other assistant can discuss the topic at length with the student. Furthermore, the student needs ample time to do some background research prior to the writing assignment. For example, if the student is writing a persuasive paper on a favorite movie, have her work on a list of favorite movies, scenes, and actors several days prior to the first day of the lesson. Then, when you start the lesson with the class, she is prepared to begin writing ideas down because she has something to aid memory recall. Since students with AS often have trouble keeping up during writing assignments, this preparatory work will help reduce the student's anxiety and help increase time on task.

Organizational tools

Most teachers use a variety of organizing and "web" techniques when beginning the writing process to help students generate ideas, and subsequently record and group those ideas. Some of these webbing strategies begin with a central theme written in the center of the paper or in the middle of the chalkboard, followed by related terms and ideas branching off from the central theme. These strategies are great tools for the neurotypical student, but some of them can be very confusing to students with AS.

It is best to use ONE type of organizational system in which the elementary student with AS lists and organizes ideas for writing assignments, regardless of the method the rest of the class is using. A strategy I have developed is the I.C.O. method, designed specifically for students with AS. This method requires the student to:

1. Create a list of *Ideas* related to the topic
2. Make a *Category Chart* to categorize and organize the ideas
3. Use an *Outline* to prepare for writing a first draft

Since the ultimate goal of the activity is to encourage students to list and organize ideas prior to writing a rough draft, they should be permitted to use an individualized method for accomplishing that task.

To begin, the student is given the topic and is assisted in preparing a list of ideas, details, and examples for the paper. Table 4.4 provides an example of an Idea List for a persuasive paper on a favorite movie director.

TABLE 4.4
Idea List for Persuasive Paper

TOPIC: Favorite movie director

My favorite movie director is: _Steven Spielberg_

Aliens	Lots of action
Attack scenes	Who will be attacked?
Sharks	Where are the attacks?
Boats	Where are the sharks?
Beach scenes	Will they be rescued?
Boys flying	Dinosaurs
Space	Rescue scenes
Robots	Heroes
Fast-moving plot	

After the list is made, the items are divided into at least three categories. Again, the student will more than likely need help with this step. One way to create the categories is to put the list of ideas on notecards with one idea, detail, or example per card. Next, the student works on grouping the cards by common features or criteria. For the list above, the categories could be *Suspense, Action,* and *Special Effects.* Figure 4.6 is an example of how the Category Chart might look.

To create the Category Chart, turn a loose-leaf sheet of paper horizontally so the lines now run vertically. Fold the paper in thirds along the vertical lines to create three equally sized columns. The student writes the category names at the top of the page, one at the top of each column. The list of ideas, details, and examples are then written in the column in which they belong (see Figure 4.6). Some students will need a great deal of guidance with this step until they gain proficiency.

Category Chart

TOPIC: Steven Spielberg's movies are the best movies ever made!

Category 1: _Suspence_   Category 2: _Action_   Category 3: _Special Effects_

Who will be attacked?   Attack scenes   Aliens

Where are the sharks?   Rescue scenes   Dinosaurs

Will they be rescued?   Fast-moving action   Robots

Beach scenes   Heroes   Boys flying

Figure 4.6. Category chart.

After the ideas have been categorized, the student fills in an outline. The outline in Figure 4.7 can be used for any writing assignment. That is, the number of details and paragraphs can be increased or decreased depending on the writing level of the student, making it useful to students in grades 2-6. Each Roman numeral on the outline represents a paragraph and each letter represents a detail within a paragraph.

The student uses the completed Category Chart to fill in the outline. First, she writes the topic or theme for the assignment at the top of the page. Then she incorporates this topic or theme into an *opening statement,* which is written next to the **I** on the outline. The student now writes the names of the three categories from her organizing chart next to the letters **A**, **B**, and **C** under Roman numeral **I**. Section **I** on the outline later becomes the introductory paragraph for the paper. Letter **D** is the transition or concluding sentence in each paragraph which may be omitted, depending on the writing level of the student. (See Figure 4.8 for a completed outline using the information from the Category Chart presented in Figure 4.6.)

OUTLINE

TOPIC/THEME _____

I. _____

        A. _____
        B. _____
        C. _____
        D. _____
            _____

II. _____

        A. _____
        B. _____
        C. _____
        D. _____
            _____

III. _____

        A. _____
        B. _____
        C. _____
        D. _____
            _____

IV. _____

        A. _____
        B. _____
        C. _____
        D. _____
            _____

V. _____
            _____

        A. _____
        B. _____
        C. _____
        D. _____
            _____

Figure 4.7. Sample outline.

The body of the paper is developed from sections **II**, **III**, and **IV**. To complete these sections on the outline, the student writes the name of the first category next to **II**, the name of the second category next to **III**, and the name of the third category next to **IV**. She then fills in letters **A**, **B**, and **C** under each Roman numeral in the outline by selecting three details from each category on the Category Chart (see Figure 4.8). (Letter **D** may be another detail, or it may serve as a transition or concluding sentence, depending on the structure of the assignment or requirements by the teacher.)

The last section on the outline, **V**, is the section from which the concluding paragraph is developed. A simple way to teach the student to fill in this section is to have her rewrite the information from section **I**. To do so, she first writes a sentence in which she restates the theme. This is written next to **V**. For letters **A**, **B**, and **C** in paragraph **V**, the student writes the three category names again. Make sure that the categories are written in the same order in which they were previously written on the outline. The last item to complete on the outline is the *closing statement.* This is written next to letter **D**, paragraph **V**, at the end of the outline. Depending on the type of paper (persuasive, expository, narrative) to be written, standard phrases can be used to complete this section. Teach students to write concluding statements using simple phrases such as those illustrated in Table 4.5. As they develop their writing skills, students will learn to generate original closing statements.

TABLE 4.5
Concluding Phrases

Persuasive: *"For these reasons, I believe that ..."*

Narrative: *"This is a time I'll never forget because ..."* or
"This is important to me because ...."

Expository: *"_____ is (was, has been, etc.) important because ...."*

OUTLINE

TOPIC/THEME Favorite movie director

I. Steven Spielberg's movies are the best movies ever made!
- **A.** Suspense
- **B.** Action
- **C.** Special effects
- **D.** Good directors know how to use suspense, action, and special effects to make movies that are fun to watch.

II. Suspense
- **A.** Who will be attacked?
- **B.** Where are the sharks?
- **C.** Where will they be rescued?
- **D.** Steven Spielberg is good at creating suspenseful movies with lots of action.

III. Action
- **A.** Attack scenes
- **B.** Fast-moving action
- **C.** Heroes
- **D.** Spielberg's movies have fast-paced action with heroes who make them fun to watch!

IV. Special Effects
- **A.** Aliens
- **B.** Dinosaurs
- **C.** Boys flying
- **D.** Spielberg's movies have won many awards because of interesting visual effects.

V. I think Steven Spielberg is the best movie director because he makes great movies.
- **A.** Suspense
- **B.** Action
- **C.** Special effects
- **D.** For these reasons, I believe Steven Spielberg is the best movie director in the world.

Figure 4.8. Completed outline.

Using a formula for writing is one of the most successful ways to teach students with AS the writing process. Figure 4.8 is an example of a completed outline for a persuasive writing assignment on a favorite movie director.

This I.C.O. strategy has been used successfully for writing narrative, persuasive, and expository papers with many students with AS. Some students dictate every word for their Idea List, Category Chart, and Outline to a paraprofessional or other assistant while others use a tape recorder or computer to complete the process. By helping to keep the student organized, this strategy creates a sense of structure when beginning the writing process.

First draft

After the outline is completed, the student begins writing the first draft. The opening statement is developed from what was written next to **I** on the outline. The rest of the paragraph is developed from the information written next to the letters **A**, **B**, **C**, and **D**. The student continues by repeating this process for each of the remaining paragraphs, such that the information included under **II** is used to develop the second paragraph of the paper, the information under **III** is used for third paragraph, and so on, until the student has completed the first draft of her paper.

Students will need guided practice until they have mastered using the Idea List, Category Chart and Outline, but once mastered, these tools will enable them to write any type of paper independently. By using the same type of organizational method for EVERY writing assignment, the student's writing skills will improve and she will develop independence at a faster rate than if several different types of prewriting activities are used.

Once students have gathered background information, formulated some ideas about the writing topic, and have received some assistance with organizing their ideas, the paper they produce can be quite good. When time constraints prohibit extra preparation time, consider reducing the length of the assignment. The difficulties students with AS experience in writing are complex, stemming from a neurological impairment, language disorder, and poorly developed motor skills.

Social Studies and Science

Note-Taking

Students with AS can become lost in the details and therefore unable to discern what is important information within the social studies or science textbook. In addition, note-taking during class lectures can seem like an insurmountable task. To accommodate for such problems, have the student read the chapter prior to the class lecture or discussion. Provide her with an outline of relevant information on which she can add details from the chapter. For example, the Half & Half note-taking strategy described in Chapter Three works well for social studies and science material. By reading the material and taking notes about it before it is presented in class, the student has to do less writing in class and is better able to follow along with the discussion. Then, during the class lecture, the student keeps his notes on his desk, and if he hears something that is not already in the notes, he adds it on the right-hand side (the class notes side of the paper; see Figure 3.12).

Cooperative Group Activites

It is common practice at the elementary level to incorporate cooperative group teaching-learning activities in social studies and science. Be prepared to offer assistance by interpreting, scripting, and prompting students with AS in these instances. This can be done by training a paraprofessional or parent volunteer to work with the student when the teacher's role prohibits her from being available to the student with AS for the entire activity. A paraprofessional stays with my son during all cooperative group activities. Thus, she is available to interpret the pragmatic language of group members, explain my son's body language or expressions to the other students so they can understand him, provide lines of dialogue and keep him from monologuing, and prompt him when it is his turn to participate or perform a specific task.

Reading Selections

Some of the social studies and science textbooks, as well as other reading materials such as *Scholastic News* or *Time for Kids*, are written above the reading level of some students with AS. When this is the case, provide the information at a level that is comfortable for the student, and, if necessary, ask the school librarian, reading specialist, paraprofessional, or parent volunteer to help you locate appropriate reading materials. Another option is to have the student sit with a peer or other volunteer who reads the information to the student, taking frequent breaks to discuss the content and reviewing the information at the end of the reading selection. (Be sure to train the peer or volunteer ahead of time in how to do this.)

Many students with AS have retained a wealth of knowledge about a particular subject while pursuing their special interests. If their special interest is related to the social studies or science topic being studied, encourage them to find additional reading material on the topic, since they may already be familiar with the material presented in class. For example, when doing a unit on bats,

> *Many students with AS have retained a wealth of knowledge about a particular subject.*

Steven was given permission to bring in books and magazine articles on bats that contained additional information for him to read because he already knew everything in the class reading selections. In cases like this, it is important to check the level of the materials the student brings in because they may not be at the student's comprehension level, as will be explored in the following section on reading skills.

Reading

Some children with AS appear to be exceptional readers, but once their comprehension level is assessed, you will often find that they do not comprehend what they are able to read aloud. Others are good readers, reading and comprehending well above grade level but choose to do nothing else but read, thereby neglecting practice in other subjects and avoiding social situations. Likewise, there are students who are excellent readers but only in one genre: nonfiction. Because nonfiction reading comprehension is based on literal recall of facts – an area of strength for many students with AS – they find this genre most rewarding and interesting. However, they struggle when required to read and comprehend fictional works, which rely on the reader to generalize and analyze the text while reading, an area of weakness for many children with AS due to problems with perspective-taking and theory of mind.

One-on-One Instruction

For the student who is hyperlexic, individual instruction is necessary in addition to group instruction. Children with AS can be quite perfectionistic. Students who decode written language far better than they comprehend it can become frustrated, embarrassed, and uncooperative when this is brought to their attention, especially in front of their peers. For this reason, they may be difficult to teach in a group setting. If this is the case, slowly introduce the student into the group setting after she has gained confidence in 1:1 reading instruction and is no longer concerned about her reading level. By working with the student 1:1 for a while, you will help her become comfortable and cooperative when assigned reading material that is truly on her comprehension level as would occur in a reading group situation.

Children with AS can be quite perfectionistic.

During the first week of school, Lexi, a first-grader with AS, told her teacher that she could read *Harry Potter* and insisted on being assigned reading material on at least a sixth-grade level. After administering an IRI (Informal Reading Inventory – an oral reading test) to assess her reading level, the teacher determined that Lexi was *not* reading on a sixth-grade level, as she had proclaimed. She was able to read aloud, that is, decode, reading material on a sixth-grade level, but she was not able to answer any comprehension questions other than a few literal recall-type questions. When the teacher formed a reading group with Lexi and four other students who read at approximately the same level as Lexi (2.5), Lexi refused to cooperate, complaining daily to her mother that the reading was too easy and that she was not going to read such childish books since she was capable of reading *Harry Potter*. The teacher worked with her individually, asking Lexi to practice her reading with the teacher *and* allowing her to read books of her choice at specific times during the day. In about a month's time, Lexi became comfortable reading the books on her true reading level and found a great deal of success in answering comprehension questions correctly, as well as enjoying stories she could understand. She began to reap the rewards of reading: finding enjoyment in the story as opposed to just being able to read the words aloud. At that point, Lexi rejoined the reading group and participated enthusiastically.

By allowing Lexi time to discover the joy of reading and becoming comfortable with her reading level, the teacher made it possible for Lexi to feel in control. Since individuals with AS have a strong need for control, this way of encouraging Lexi to cooperate proved very successful. By the end of the school year, she no longer insisted on reading material that was above her comprehension level, participated fully in her reading group, and chose independent reading material on her level.

Advanced Readers

Some students with AS read above grade level. These students are often so absorbed in reading that they miss opportunities for social experiences. Encourage their reading but use it as a means to develop social skills, for example, by having another good reader in the class read the same book as the student with AS and allow them to do a project together related to the book. For instance, assign the students to read a book such as *My Side of the Mountain* and to complete a project such as making a map of the Catskill Mountains where the main character, Sam, lives, or constructing a model of Sam's tree-stump house described in the book. The partners will need monitoring, and the student with AS will need assistance in navigating through the social aspects of the joint project, such as reminding him to ask for input from his partner or "interpeting" pragmatics and colloquial terms like "Do you think it will fly?" Nevertheless, such an arrangement provides a natural context in which the student can display his proficiency at reading and develop social skills at the same time.

Reading Comprehension

Many students with AS comprehend nonfiction material extremely well, but are significantly less proficient at comprehending fictional material that requires inferencing, generalizing, or analyzing. When first assessing a student's reading level, it is important to accurately analyze her ability to draw conclusions, generalize beyond the text, compare and contrast, make predictions based on given information, and discern between facts and opinions. Most basal reading series provide tests for this type of assessment. Other diagnostic reading tools include:

> **Many students with AS comprehend nonfiction material extremely well.**

- *Stanford Diagnostic Reading Test, Fourth Edition* (SDRT 4) published by Harcourt
- *Gates-MacGinitie Reading Tests, Fourth Edition* (GMRT) published by Riverside Publishing, a division of Houghton Mifflin
- *Reading Skills Series: Comprehension* published by Steck-Vaughn
- *Reading Placement Tests* published by Scholastic

Reading comprehension can also be assessed using teacher-, school-, district-, or state-created tests. Cloze tasks, which require the student to fill in words where systematic deletions have been made in a passage, and narrative comprehension tasks, which are authentic measures of emergent readers' comprehension skills that require retelling of story elements, are also useful tools for assessing reading comprehension. Furthermore, authentic assessments such as anecdotal records, interviews, and portfolios can be used.

In some cases, a reading specialist may be needed in order to accurately assess a student's comprehension level. The first-grade student who can tell you everything you ever wanted to know about telescopes and constellations may in reality be comprehending at a first- or second-grade level, but adults who do not know her well may think she reads and comprehends at a much higher level. It is important to know the difference and identify where gaps between comprehension and word-calling ability exist so appropriate assistance can be provided, such as frequent 1:1 reading instruction sessions where the student is taught how to read text for information and a purpose rather than simply for word calling.

Some students with AS need frequent, direct instruction in drawing conclusions, generalizing beyond the text, making comparisons and predictions, and distinguishing between fact and fiction. You may need to use reading material that is very basic, just as you would for a beginning reader. Although they may have spent hours upon hours reading, they may not have developed the ability to comprehend text, as typical readers do who spend hours reading.

When the responsibility of providing direct instruction for students with AS falls on the teacher, she may need access to materials not typically provided for her grade level. World Teachers Press publishes two series of books that use cloze tasks to teach comprehension: *Cloze Encounters* (McGuinnes, 2000) and *Cloze In On Language* (Moore, 1998). These series are especially useful for students with AS because they are available at a variety of levels and the text is large and widely spaced, making it easy for students to read, fill in blanks, and answer questions. The books are also easy for teachers to use since every page is reproducible and answer keys are provided. In addition to cloze tasks, the *Cloze Encounters* series contains reading passages followed by reading comprehension pages incorporating literal, inferential, and evaluative questions. The *Cloze In On Language* series contains cloze tests with answers provided in a word bank at the end and activities designed to develop vocabulary, an understanding of story line, and an awareness of context clues.

A useful guide for planning and implementing an individualized reading program is *Individualized Reading: A Complete Guide for Managing One-On-One Instruction* (English, 1996). This book provides suggestions and guidelines for the following:

- Daily schedule
- Informal reading inventories
- Initial assessment
- Placement
- Mini-lessons
- Response journals
- Cross-curriculum integration
- Final assessment

- Time management
- Running records
- Authentic assessment
- Assessing progress
- Student-selection techniques
- Student-teacher conferences
- Student motivation
- Meeting with next-year teachers

It is comprehensive in scope and provides practical, easy-to-use strategies like the Story Puzzle (English, 1996). Before beginning the Story Puzzle activity, English suggests writing a fairy tale that is missing one story element such as characters, setting, plot, problem, or solution. (I have found that this can also be accomplished by reading a story/book that is unfamiliar to the students rather than taking the time to write an original story.)

To begin the activity with the student, review story elements and write them on a brightly colored poster board labeled Story Parts (or Story Elements). Next, tell the student that you are making a puzzle and cut the board apart so that each story element is a separate piece of the puzzle. After that, remove one piece of the puzzle and ask the student to assemble the puzzle. As the student is assembling the puzzle, emphasize that it is incomplete since one element is missing. Tell him that it is easy to understand stories when you can find all the story elements, just as it is easy to build the puzzle when you have all the pieces. Last, read the fairy tale, or other story you have selected, leaving out one of the story elements. Help the student identify which element is missing. As a follow-up activity, I recommend having the student repeat the process with the teacher. In other words, the student chooses a story, removes a particular element, and the teacher has to identify the missing story element. By doing this, the student must focus on story elements, thus reinforcing the Story Puzzle lesson with a fun activity.

Another successful technique for teaching comprehension through the study of story parts is to use Goal Structure Story Maps found in *Helping the Struggling Reader: What to Teach and How to Teach It* (Sundbye & McCoy, 2001). The authors recommend that this strategy be used with students who have difficulty answering questions about stories, in particular, inferential and evaluative. There are four components to the map: (a) a main character's name, (b) the goal (what the character wants to do or have), (c) the attempt (what the character did to reach the goal), and (d) the outcome of the attempt (yes or no answer).

Before using the strategy with a reading selection, the student practices it by "mapping" a real-life incident. For example, Marianna wants to stay up late to watch a television program on insects. She puts all her books and toys away in her room. Because she cleaned her room when her mother asked her, Marianna was allowed to watch the program. For this story, the four story map components are:

(a) Character: Marianna
(b) Goal: Watch a program on insects
(c) Attempt: Clean her room
(d) Outcome: Yes

This process can be repeated for the other person in the story as well – the mother. In that case, the four story map components would be:

(a) Character: Marianna's mother
(b) Goal: Have Marianna clean her room
(c) Attempt: Ask Marianna to clean her room
(d) Outcome: Yes

Students with AS will find this strategy useful because it is short, systematic, and predictable. However, as seen with the second story map, inferential thinking is required in order to complete the map. Therefore, provide clues and ask questions to help guide students to find all the components needed to complete story maps that are difficult.

The strategy can be used with students of all ages, as the terminology can be simplified to make it easier for young children. To take the strategy to a higher, more complex level, Sundbye and McCoy suggest that character relationships as well as cause-effect relationships be explored. This is done by examining how characters' actions impact each other's goals, attempts, and outcomes.

Students with AS need more practice in acquiring newly practiced skills as they generally have trouble applying them to novel situations, even if the difference is slight. For example, the student may be able to discern fact from fiction in one book but not in another, even though the same instructions and routine were followed. Difficulty generalizing information is a major characteristic of individuals with AS. Their learning tends to be situation-/context-dependent as opposed to learning that complements and is adjusted to previously acquired knowledge. For this reason, they take longer to acquire new skills and need a great deal more time practicing new skills. Frequent, direct reading instruction is often the best way to help students with AS who comprehend text at a significantly lower level than they word call, which is often the case when they are required to read fictional material.

> *Students with AS need more practice in acquiring newly practiced skills.*

Reading Aloud

Reading aloud in front of classmates is very difficult for some students with AS. These students are easy to identify – they are visibly nervous or simply refuse to read aloud. Consider excusing such students from reading aloud until they are comfortable doing so. Do not force them. Over time and with support, they usually gain confidence and feel less self-conscious about reading aloud.

There are many ways to help a student overcome feelings of anxiety. These include:

- having the student observe classmates reading aloud for a period of time before being asked to do so themselves
- forming a group of two, which includes the student with AS and a peer from the class, who then practice reading aloud
- offering rewards for any attempt at reading aloud, even if it is just with the teacher without anyone else in the room

Another successful technique consists of asking the student to read one word aloud intermittently as the teacher reads aloud from a book. This is done by unexpectedly stopping your reading aloud at a point in the story where it would be easy to fill in the blank. Because students with AS typically are impulsive, they tend to "fill in the blank" if you unexpectedly stop reading aloud mid-sentence. If you want to hear the student's voice, this works best in a small-group setting. In a larger group, there may be too many children who fill in the blank so you won't be able to hear the student with AS. If you continue to offer positive feedback while using this fill-in-the-blank strategy, the student will begin to feel comfortable speaking and reading aloud in front of her peers.

The skill of reading aloud in front of others is important throughout life. The student will be called upon throughout her schooling to speak in front of people. In the workplace, this skill is also valuable for sharing ideas with colleagues or discussing performance with a supervisor. The opportunities and achievements students experience in reading aloud at school will help them develop the confidence they need to tackle other obstacles in their lives.

Spelling/Vocabulary

As with reading, spelling and vocabulary can be great sources of anxiety and/or frustration for students with AS. Adjusting the curriculum and individualizing spelling and vocabulary instruction and assessment help these students perform up to their potential.

Spelling

For students who are perfectionistic (as many students with AS are), the spelling pretest is often a source of great anxiety. If the goal of spelling assignments is to ensure that students master a list of words, then try to eliminate the pretest for students who cannot handle it and give them a different assignment using the same words while the rest of the class takes the test. Another means of reducing anxiety over spelling pretests is to give the student the words a few days before the test so she can study them at home ahead of time. This way the student is less anxious about the pretest and can participate with the rest of the class. A third means of reducing anxiety is to allow the student to spell words aloud instead of writing them down. Regardless of the method you choose, remember that it serves no purpose to force an anxious student to take a pretest that does not affect grades or demonstrate mastery of the list.

If the student can spell a majority of the words for the unit, try offering her a challenge list as a way to keep her motivated and on task. The student may also create a list of unfamiliar words she wants to spell. Encourage students to learn the meaning of the spelling words in addition to just memorizing the spelling.

When spelling and vocabulary lists are created from students' work and classroom materials such as reading books, textbooks, periodicals, and the like, success at learning them is usually improved. For students with AS, consider creating alternative lists if they are not successful at learning the lists provided in grade-level workbooks.

Vocabulary

When teaching vocabulary, it is best to teach the words in the context of a story or article. Students with AS are generally good at memorizing facts, but they sometimes have difficulty comprehending and using the bits of information they have stored in their memory. If the vocabulary words are

It is best to teach the words in the context of a story or article.

taught in the context of a story or article, the student is better able to form a mental image of the concepts related to the words. This is a particularly successful technique for teaching vocabulary, since people with AS are visual thinkers.

Dictation

Dictation tests are usually difficult for students with AS as many have trouble processing the auditory information quickly enough to coordinate their motor planning and accommodate for their dysgraphia as they try to write down what they hear. Before starting, determine what the goal for the dictation is. If it is just to see if the student knows how to spell the list words, then excuse the student with AS from the dictation portion of the test. During dictation, ask the student with AS to do a different type of assessment using the list words, such as a fill-in-the blank section that would include sentences with the list word missing and the list words provided in a word bank on the test. If, on the other hand, the goal is to test the student's ability to take dictation, find another setting and method that is more appropriate for the student. For example, work with the student privately or have him work with a paraprofessional in a quiet location.

Special Classes: Art, Music, Gym

Any change in teaching style, classroom expectations, and room arrangement can be confusing for students with AS and result in inappropriate behaviors as well as poor performance. It is important to carefully analyze the dynamics of the special classes and make adjustments, where necessary, for the unique characteristics of students with AS. Be sure to give the student a tour of the room, put expectations and rules in writing, and give the student time to adjust to the teaching style of the various special-subject teachers.

Some students with AS have trouble remembering where to sit in classes they attend just once a week. For those students, place a sticker on their chair and be sure to remind them to sit where the sticker is. Because many students with AS do not like others to be in their personal space, some may need a seat at the end of a row, table, or group of desks; others many need to sit alone to function best in the special classes. My son was not able to concentrate on lessons when he was seated with children on both sides of him. He spent the class periods trying to avoid being touched by other students or by trying to keep their pencils, scissors and other belongings away from him. When his teachers moved him to the end of a row, his attention and time on task improved significantly.

One of the best ways to help a child with AS adjust to change and differences in routines is to use visuals such as written schedules, Option Cards, and checklists. Specific examples of visuals are presented in each of the following sections: art, music, and gym.

Art

The student with AS may have difficulty in art class for a number of reasons, in addition to more universal problems. First, she may have fine-motor problems, making it difficult for her to draw, cut, paint, or work with clay. Second, she may have sensory problems that cause her to avoid touching certain textures or substances, especially sticky and wet materials.

Checklists in art class help students with AS remember the rules for gathering and using supplies, as well as returning them at the end of the period. Since art class is typically only once a week, the student may have trouble remembering not only the rules for supplies, but also the routine for taking attendance, how to request assistance, or where to sit. Therefore, provide the student with visual supports. Begin with a checklist for supplies. Make it as brief and simply stated as possible and include pictures for students who cannot read. Table 4.6 shows an example of a checklist for art.

TABLE 4.6
Art Supplies Checklist

1. Take 2 drawing pencils and 4 sheets of paper to ☐
   your art table.

2. If your pencils need to be sharpened, use the ☐
   teacher's sharpener.

3. When the teacher tells you to stop drawing, return ☐
   your pencils to the bin.

An Option Card can be used for situations such as requesting assistance or finding something to do when the project is completed early, as seen in Figure 4.9.

I have finished my project.

- I can use a pencil to draw on some white paper.

- I can look at an art book at my desk.

Figure 4.9. Option card for art class.

Finally, if an assistant, volunteer, or paraprofessional is available, he or she can help remind the student of classroom rules, assist with projects, and help the student interact with peers when the project requires a cooperative effort.

Music

Hearing sensitivity is very common in children with AS. Inform the music teacher ahead of time if this is the case, because the student may cover his ears, cry, or try to leave the class when hearing music. As the student becomes familiar with the music teacher and the class, he will usually begin to adjust.

Another problem involves frequent changes in routine. One week the children stay in their seats and listen to recorded music and/or watch a video about a composer or a section of the orchestra; another week, they do a movement activity to a piece of music; and yet another week, they practice for an upcoming musical where they are required to stay in one spot for an extended period of time. Such frequent change, or lack of routine, can be very confusing to children with AS. Unlike their neurotypical peers who look forward to the exciting variety of activities in music class, the student with AS can become frustrated, anxious, and angry. Provide the student with AS visual support in the form of a schedule that includes exactly what will take place during the class as well as student expectations. Table 4.7 is an example of such a schedule. Now the student knows exactly what will happen during the entire class period and what is expected of her. This schedule can be given to her the day before class, sent home the night before, or given to her the morning before the class so she has time to prepare and ask questions prior to going to music.

Clearly, not all situations can be so explicitly defined, and there will be times when the schedule must change. For that reason, a reminder is always written at the bottom of the schedule: *Remember: Sometimes the schedule changes!* If a change is going to take place, try to offer the student some extra assistance and provide a Change in Routine Card (see Figure 3.1). Have a volunteer or paraprofessional explain what is happening and help the student adjust to the change by writing down what the change will be or

TABLE 4.7
Schedule for Music Class

Music Schedule for Wed., May 15

Today we will be learning about <u>string instruments</u>.

1. Go to the seat with the yellow sticker on it.
2. Stay in your seat while we listen to two pieces of music.
3. The music teacher wants you to listen to the music and not talk.
4. After you listen to music, the teacher will play two instruments, one at a time, and then tell you about the instruments.
5. The music teacher wants you to listen without talking while he plays the instruments.
6. After he tells you about the instruments, you can raise your hand to ask questions about the music or the instruments.
7. After the teacher answers questions, he will tell you to line up at the door.
8. Wait in line until your teacher comes to the door.
9. Do not touch other people while you are in line.
10. When the teacher comes to the door, you will stay in line and walk back to your class.

Remember: Sometimes the schedule changes!

having her meet the substitute teacher, for example, before class begins. These strategies help the child with AS adjust to classroom and teacher expectations, deal with the unexpected, and enable her too participate in class with her peers.

Gym

Gym class usually presents problems for students with AS. For example, many have motor-planning problems and difficulty timing their motor movements. They may also have trouble following the teacher's verbal instructions and body movements. In addition, the loud noise in the gym can be painful, and the chaos they perceive in the midst of an activity may be overwhelming and frustrating. Under such pressure, students with AS often exhibit atypical behaviors, sometimes causing other students to avoid or provoke them.

Because the pace in gym class can be quite rapid, it may be necessary to have a paraprofessional or adaptive P.E. teacher assist the student in keeping up and help him avoid becoming overwhelmed and confused. Some children become so overwhelmed that they break down, cry, or refuse to participate. If possible, have someone serve as a coach to prompt the student when and where to move, remind him of game rules, and intercede when verbal exchanges are misinterpreted.

The student with AS may also need visual supports during the class such as colored cards that are cues for specific actions; for example, a red card to remind him to stop, a green card to remind him to go, or a blue card to remind him that it is time to line up at the door. Visual cues are easier for him to comprehend than verbal commands at times when anxiety is high and/or when a great deal of activity is taking place. Work with the gym teacher, the paraprofessional, and the parents to determine a color card system that will work for the student.

Frequently, students with AS are victims of bullying. Bullying often takes place in the gym class, where students tend to work under less teacher supervision and because it is a place where some of the awkward social and motor characteristics of students with AS become particularly prominent.

Kieran, a third-grade student with AS, had difficulty in gym because of his poor gross-motor skills, inability to imitate the movements demonstrated by the teacher, weak upper body, lack of experience in organized sports such as basketball or baseball, lack of understanding of game rules, and difficulty following verbal instructions. At the annual review of his IEP, the P.E. teacher provided a detailed narrative of every skill or objective Kieran should have met by grade 3 and a list of recommendations to improve his motor skills, which included 1:1 adaptive PE services and assistance during gym class. The P.E. teacher was very concerned that as the years passed, Kieran would not be able to participate in gym with his class unless his needs were addressed and assistance was provided. She also knew that he was at risk for teasing and ridicule by bullies. Her honest and detailed description of Kieran's motor problems provided valuable information for the IEP team. As a result of changes made to his IEP, Kieran made great strides the following year with additional services and assistance. He learned to jump rope, catch a ball from both a close distance and far away, and dribble a basketball – all skills that most 9-year-olds have mastered. He also gained confidence in his newly developed abilities and became less anxious during the regular gym class.

In some cases, it may be necessary to place the student in an alternative setting, offer OT and adaptive P.E. services, or provide an assistant during the gym class to accommodate for the special needs of the student with AS.

So far, organizational supports and academic accommodations for ensuring successful performance of students with AS have been discussed. In the next chapter, we will look at how social problems can be addressed and offer strategies for dealing with these problems.

CHAPTER FIVE

Developing Social Skills

U niversally, individuals with AS have different social characteristics than their neurotpyical peers. Specifically, they tend
to fall outside the norm in their manner of speaking, use of
body language, and understanding of accepted social codes of behavior. Further, they do not know how to interpret or use nonverbal
communication. Unexpected changes/occurrences and crowded,
noisy environments cause their anxiety levels to escalate rapidly.
Furthermore, their resistance to change and their rigid thinking style
make it difficult, if not impossible, to adjust to the quick-paced, con-
tinually changing exchanges that take place during social interactions. Needless to say, this puts them at a disadvantage in social settings and situations where they must interact with others, especially
their peers.

Fortunately, many strategies and specially designed programs
have been found effective for improving the social skills of students
with AS. In this chapter, the issue of anxiety is first addressed.
Before any lasting learning can take place, anxiety, which is a major
problem for individuals with AS, needs to be controlled. After a
general introduction, a series of particularly anxiety-provoking

situations will be discussed along with interventions for handling them. Next, difficult moments (Myles & Southwick, 1999) are addressed along with recommendations for prevention and intervention. In the subsequent section, the importance of play and its role in social skills development is discussed, followed by social skills instruction including:

- *I Can Say* – a strategy for teaching social language
- Social Language Groups – a method for teaching reciprocal communication skills
- Social Stories – a strategy for managing social situations
- SOCCSS – a strategy for developing an understanding of social situations and developing problem-solving skills
- *Friends for Me* – a social skills program for developing friendships skills

Before you begin assisting children with AS in social situations, it is important to develop an understanding of their problems due to anxiety and the difficulty they experience controlling their emotions and behaviors.

Anxiety

One of the greatest problems for students with AS is anxiety. The anxiety can be mild or it can be severely debilitating. Whatever the intensity, it must be considered and diminished before any lasting learning can take place. This means that the entire team, including teachers, social worker, psychologist, occupational therapist, parents, and the student, must work together to identify the sources of anxiety and make a plan to reduce it.

As discussed in earlier chapters, most students with AS have difficulty accepting changes in the daily schedule and any rearrangement of the classroom and materials. Surprises such as a substitute teacher or a fire alarm can cause them so much distress and anxiety that they are unable to focus on schoolwork and maintain composure for the rest of the day (Myles & Adreon, 2001; Myles & Southwick, 1999). These unexpected events can be as simple as a change in the number of problems to complete in a math assignment or the teacher taking attendance visually one day rather than calling out each child's name. Whenever possible, discuss changes in the routine or environment before they occur. Prepare the student and allow her time to accept the change by giving her a copy of the schedule changes or a floor plan of the new class arrangement a day ahead of time; sooner if possible. The leading cause of anxiety for these children is an <u>unexpected</u> event or change in plans. A calm, content student can quickly explode when encountering something unexpected.

> *The leading cause of anxiety for these children is an unexpected event or change in plans.*

Write a <u>list</u> of known *triggers* that set off the student, such as unexpected loud sounds or someone touching her desk. Talk to the student's parents, siblings, and former teachers when generating the list. In addition to other teachers, be sure to share the list with staff members so they will understand the student's behaviors and reactions when they encounter the student on the playground, in the hall, or at lunch in the cafeteria.

It is important to remember that even though you are able to identify anxiety triggers and develop a plan for reducing the student's anxiety, the student may still experience heightened levels of anxiety and will need systematic and rehearsed preparation to help her learn to adjust both to social demands and her own problems with anxiety. The following is a discussion of situations that occur before, during, and after the school day that cause students with AS the greatest amount of anxiety.

- Getting ready for school
- Entering the building
- Sitting close to others
- Keeping up with classmates
- Struggling with difficult work
- Answering direct questions
- Dealing with sarcasm
- Making eye contact
- Receiving a group grade
- Interacting with peers

- Eating in the cafeteria
- Navigating through unstructured times (recess and free-choice)
- Adjusting to change
- Attending assemblies
- Having a substitute teacher
- Exiting during a fire drill
- Going on a field trip
- Arriving home

Getting Ready for School

Mornings are often anxious times for students with AS. The activities involved in preparing to leave the house can be stressful. Eating breakfast in a timely manner, finding their clothing and shoes, and packing their backpacks are all anxiety-provoking for many students with AS. Encourage parents to develop a structured routine for their child. They should try to keep the child on a schedule, with a routine for getting up, dressing, eating breakfast, brushing teeth, gathering belongings, and leaving the house. Such a routine helps the student relax, knowing that he will arrive at school on time and with all of his belongings.

Before my son was diagnosed with AS, we did not have a morning routine. We got up at varying times, dressed before eating some days while eating before dressing on others. We often ran frantically around the house, searching for shoes, books, homework, and notes to be signed. Then we would run to the car, zipping coats along the way. When we arrived at the school, I would give my son instructions about taking the bus home after school or waiting for me to pick him up as he dashed out the car, papers flying out of his backpack, and scurried off to class right before the bell rang. Shortly after my son's diagnosis and learning about AS, I realized that he needed a morning routine so he would leave the house feeling relaxed and ready to tackle the obstacles that awaited him at school. By not having a morning routine, he started school each day with his anxiety level already elevated. This is not how a student with AS should begin his day!

Entering the Building

When entering the school building, students with AS are among many talking, moving people, which can cause them to feel closed in and overwhelmed. The noise of backpacks dropping, lunch boxes being placed on the floor, people talking, bells ringing, and doors closing is difficult for them to tolerate. The halls and classrooms appear chaotic with students moving rapidly from one place to another. By the time the student gets to his desk, his anxiety level has all ready begun to rise.

Make a list of the sounds and activities that are difficult for the student and offer visuals such as a Morning Checklist, Daily Schedule, and Option Cards (see Chapter Three) to help him stay focused and independent while preparing for the start of the school day. If the student is not able to cope with the anxiety he experiences when entering the school, seek permission for him to enter the building a few minutes before other students arrive. This accommodation, in combination with a morning routine at home, has notably helped reduce my son's anxiety level at school, thereby enabling him to better deal with change, interact with peers, and perform well academically. Adult supervision is necessary when students enter the building early, so you will also need to find someone to escort the student to the room and stay with him until the teacher arrives.

Sitting Close to Others

Students with AS often experience feelings of anxiety within the classroom. This can be due to a number of causes. For example, close proximity to people can be very distracting and uncomfortable for them. As recommended in Chapter Three, give the student time to adjust to the classroom environment by allowing him to sit alone or with one other child at first. Remember that the student's perception of sensory stimuli can be hypersensitive, so be alert to signs that the student is reacting to discomfort from sensory overload. Generally, the student will exhibit behaviors reflecting his level of discomfort and anxiety such as hand-biting, rocking, humming, scratching, withdrawal, and so on. It is important to have created a list of triggers and already be familiar with the student's signs of distress before school begins as his anxiety can otherwise escalate into behaviors that are difficult to manage.

The constant social contact at school is a significant source of anxiety for many students with AS. When my son has reached his limit of being near people, he now says, "I need a break from society." At school, he has the following options:

- If sitting with a group away from his desk, return to his desk
- If sitting at his desk, go to a quiet corner of the room and read
- If in a special class, go back to his regular class or stay with the paraprofessional or inclusion facilitator
- If he needs to be alone, go to the inclusion facilitator's office (his home base)

Some students with AS use a study carrel to separate themselves from other students. This small, private space allows them to gain control and feel more relaxed. If study carrels are not available, tri-fold project display boards (available at most stores where teacher supplies are sold) work just as well. Besides, they are portable so they can be used on a desk, table, or floor, and easily moved to any room.

Keeping up with Classmates

Similarly stressful for the student with AS is the expectation that he can keep up with the class when the activity or task requires writing, for example. Many students with AS have poor-fine motor skills, hypotonia, and visual-motor difficulties. For this reason, they are unable to copy notes off the board or projection screen accurately, quickly write down what the teacher has said, or be ready to go on to the next step when the rest of the class is ready to move on. Students with AS are often aware of their inability to keep up with the class and become anxious, even before the activity or lesson begins. Providing assisitive technology, a paraprofessional or volunteer to do the writing, or allowing the student to tape the lesson can help relieve his feelings of anxiety. As mentioned, gym is another class where the pressure to keep up is particularly keen for students with AS due to poor motor coordination, and so on.

Struggling with Difficult Work

Work that is too difficult for the student results in elevated anxiety as well. Some students with AS are unable to tell their teachers that they are having trouble, and begin to exhibit anxious behaviors. Myles and Southwick (1999) refer to this as the rumbling stage. The observant teacher will recognize signs of anxiety and try to determine the precursors for these behaviors as well as options for relieving the anxiety. After talking calmly with the student, the teacher may be able to determine that the student has not understood an assignment or has misunderstood directions. At this point, she can offer assistance or clarify directions, thus diffusing the problem.

Teachers may find that on some days the student has little or no trouble with work, but on other days is incapable of doing similar work. I have interviewed many teachers who find this frustrating, but I encourage them to be patient. I have found that many children with AS, including my own, have days where everything seems to be difficult, despite accommodations. On those days, they need extra emotional support and encouragement and a reduction in the workload. With this extra support, they generally get through their day without incident and are ready to tackle their schoolwork again the following day.

Many children with AS have days where everything seems to be difficult, despite accommodations.

Answering Direct Questions

Direct questioning can also be anxiety-provoking for students with AS, who may have difficulty recalling the necessary information to answer the question or feel uncomfortable when people are looking at him. Allow the student additional time to formulate his thoughts. Furthermore, asking a student with AS *why* he did something is extremely anxiety-provoking because (a) he may have difficulty verbally describing his behavior or actions or (b) he thinks you are angry with him and feels threatened by your question. Avoid this type of direct questioning and use another approach. For example, ask the student what he wants or if he needs help rather than asking him *why* he is doing something. If warranted, this can be followed by stating a rule that relates to a situation. It is important not to confront him at this time, as this could cause him to enter the rage cycle.

When Marianna feels hot, she begins touching and hitting children nearby. Asking her to explain why she is hitting the other children only leads to more hitting and then yelling, but asking her what she needs gives her the opportunity to say, "I need some cold water. I am hot!" Marianna feels very anxious when she is hot, reacts to that feeling by striking other children, and has difficulty expressing herself when she is in this state. Therefore, she needs questions presented in a specific manner. Neurotypical children would generally answer the two questions (i.e., *Why are you doing that?* and *What do you need?*) in the same way. But that is not the case for students with AS.

Dealing with Sarcasm

Many neurotypical children find sarcasm amusing and have no trouble interpreting it. However, children with AS often do not understand it and feel humiliated when sarcastic comments are directed toward them, sometimes causing them to engage in inappropriate behavior or withdrawal. Therefore, it is best to avoid sarcasm, especially anything that can be interpreted as ridicule.

Jake's teacher remarked one day in class that Jake was "out to lunch." Jake felt humiliated because he knew the teacher was saying something negative about him, even though he was not familiar with the idiom. As a result, he refused to speak in class for fear that the teacher would humiliate him again. Rather than making a sarcastic comment to coerce Jake to pay attention in class, the teacher should have spoken privately with him about this concern.

Making Eye Contact

Forcing a student with AS to look directly at a speaker is difficult and can cause anxiety. Eye contact is not the only means by which students' attention should be assessed. Checking for understanding by having the student restate what the speaker is saying or answer a relevant question is a better option for many students with AS.

When trying to concentrate on what a speaker is saying, my son, like many other individuals with AS, casts his glance to the side of the speaker's face or watches the speaker's mouth. When casually engaged in conversation, his eye contact is better, but he is never forced to make eye contact at school, as this would increase his anxiety, hampering his ability to perform up to his potential.

Receiving a Group Grade

Group projects that result in a group grade, rather than individual student assessment, cause anxiety for some students with AS, who worry about what their partners are doing and therefore have difficulty focusing on their own work. Some are so anxious they fail to participate or become angry with the other group members. When teachers are unaware that this is a source of anxiety, they frequently see the student's behavior as immature or unreasonable and sometimes punish students with AS for their supposed resistance to work with the group. If students with AS become anxious over group work, grade them individually. This will help them stay in control, feel less anxious, and benefit from the experience of working with their peers.

Interacting with Peers

When attempting to interact with peers, students with AS are not always successful and often experience or exhibit any of the following behaviors.

- Become dictatorial or dominating when involved in play
- Demonstrate rude or aggressive behavior when their solitude is disturbed
- Stand too close to others or walk right through a game in progress without regard for the other children because they do not understand personal space rules
- Unable to keep up with changes and shifts in play and conversations, perseverating on a particular topic
- Appear disinterested because of their limited eye contact and facial expressions

- Have interests that are unusual compared to those of their peers (i.e., a 9-year-old student with AS may prefer to talk about maritime history when all the other children are talking about Pokémon)
- Quit or have tantrums when losing a game
- Adhere too rigidly to rules, alienating their peers
- Tell their peers that they do not want to play, when, in fact, they want to but are not able to say so

These behaviors may lead to social rejection and lowered self-esteem, again resulting in increased anxiety levels.

In *Helping the Child Who Doesn't Fit In* (1992), Nowicki and Duke describe this as a "terrible burden" that becomes increasingly more harmful as the child gets older. Willey, author and an individual with AS, asks "Does anyone from the NT (neurotypical) world realize the pain that can come from walking against the grain?" (Willey, 2001, p. 104). Many children with AS know they are different but have no idea how to fit in with their peers. This can have a significant psychological and emotional impact.

Angry or confused by what they see as an odd, controlling or aloof attitude, peers may avoid students with AS or make them the targets of bullying. As frequent victims of teasing and bullying, it is no wonder that many students with AS fear interacting with peers. Indeed, their anxiety can be so great that they become physically ill, withdraw completely, or have TRMs when put into social situations. School staff must address these problems by identifying and controlling students who are bullying, providing adult supervision during social situations, and teaching social skills to students with AS.

> *. . . Their anxiety can be so great that they become physically ill, withdraw completely, or have TRMs.*

Eating in the Cafeteria

For some children with AS, the cafeteria is not the fun and exciting place it is for most other children. The noise, crowds, confusing social exchanges, and smells may be overwhelming. Just imagine how you would feel if you were in a crowded elevator full of people eating their lunches and conversing loudly. This is a simple analogy of how many persons with AS experience the cafeteria on a daily basis! The following are some options for the lunch break:

- Allow the student to eat in another supervised room with a few other peers.
- Have the student sit at the end of the table in the cafeteria.
- Form a lunch buddy group that eats lunch together in the same location.
- Invite the student to have lunch with the teacher.

Because students with AS have difficulty with pragmatic language, their social skills are usually weak. The lunch break provides an excellent opportunity for a teacher or social skills facilitator to meet with the student and a peer group to work on social skills and anxiety management. Teachers who have generously periodically shared their lunch break with students have found the experience rewarding for everybody involved – the student with AS, the other students, and the teachers themselves.

Each opportunity you take to help students with AS will make a difference in their lives. You may not notice it at first, but eventually the gifts of time and reassurance will make a difference and will be truly appreciated.

Navigating Through Unstructured Times (Recess and Free-Choice Time)

Due to their struggle to understand social cues and their lack of social and emotional reciprocity, unstructured or less structured times at school can be extremely difficult for children with AS. They become anxious when they do not know what to expect or do not understand game rules during recess or free-choice time. Close monitoring and supervision is necessary, not only to assist with social interactions but to protect students with AS who have poor negotiating skills and lack confidence. For example, paraprofessionals may be assigned "recess duty" to organize and facilitate play and serve as a social coach or interpreter, guiding the child with AS.

At recess, Kim's paraprofessional stays with him, explaining games and their rules, and walking with him when he feels afraid and tries to flee from flying balls and running children. In general, she provides him with a sense of comfort since he knows she will stay with him during this chaotic time. The paraprofessional also helps Kim exit recess or free-choice time when he has become too anxious and overwhelmed by the lack of structure.

Another way to provide support for students with AS is to organize a parent volunteer group to interact with the children at recess. For example, volunteers set up game stations, craft tables, and various sports, and lead and monitor the activities. To be successful, volunteers need to be trained in how to work with students with AS; have support until they become familiar with the characteristics, behaviors, and problems related to AS; and be assisted by a staff member in planning and preparing activities.

Adult-supervised and -directed recess activities help eliminate many of the anxiety-provoking situations that can occur at recess such as fighting over balls, arguing about space, teasing and bullying, and rejection. This benefits many children, not only those with AS, by providing structure and adult facilitation.

Adjusting to Change

Changes in routine cause major anxiety for students with AS. As soon as possible, alert the student to the change by giving him a Change in Routine Card (see Figure 3.1) or some other type of visual to let him know what is happening. This simple accommodation helps the student function better for the rest of the day. Without it, he may not be able to participate on any level, withdrawing completely or having a meltdown.

Individuals with AS are rigid thinkers, making it extremely difficult for them to take somebody else's perspective, adjust to change, or accommodate for another person's needs or beliefs. In order to function within the school setting, these students need *flexibility training*. To fully reap the many rewards it has to offer, flexibility training should be carried out both at home and at school. When the strategy is only implemented in one setting, it can be difficult for the student to learn how to think flexibly. Consistency and repeated practice help these children learn new skills.

One way to teach flexibility is to use a Flexibility Chart (see Figure 5.1) and reward system.

Flexibility Chart
I will put my book away when silent reading time ends.

Monday	Tuesday	Wednesday	Thursday	Friday
	☺ 1	☺ 2	☺ 3	☺ 4
☺ 7	☺ 8	☺ 9	☺ 10	☺ 11
☺ 14	☺ 15	☺ 16	☺ 17	☺ 18
☺ 21	☺ 22	☺ 23	☺ 24	☺ 25
☺ 28	☺ 29	☺ 30		

Figure 5.1. Flexibility chart with stickers.

Flexibility training can be used to teach students to transition from one activity to another or to cope with unexpected change. Before beginning the training, choose a target behavior such as transition from silent reading to math or controlling emotions when the daily routine changes.

When in second grade, Richard had difficulty transitioning from silent reading to any other activity. He would read the same book over and over, and cry or withdraw when asked to put the book away. In addition, he often had a meltdown once he got home, frustrated that he had not been permitted to read his favorite book all day at school. To teach Richard how to transition, his teacher and parents used flexibility training. To begin, they met with Richard to explain that they wanted to help him learn to stop a favorite activity and move on to another activity. The teacher wrote the following on the top of a Flexibility Chart: *I will put my book away when silent reading time ends.* Next, she showed Richard the Flexibility Chart with the target behavior written on the back. She then told him that he would receive a sticker to place on the chart every time he complied with the rule to put his book away at the end of silent reading. Finally, she asked Richard and his mother to suggest a reward to be given to Richard when he completed the chart. They decided upon 15 minutes of computer time, one of Richard's favorite activities, to be given during a free-choice period.

The following day, Richard's teacher placed the Flexibility Chart and a picture of a computer on his desk as she asked the class to put away their books and take out their math books. The teacher looked at Richard, touched the Flexibility Chart and then the picture, and stood next to Richard for several minutes while he slowly closed his book, put it in his desk, and took out his math book. Although it took him longer than the rest of the class to make the transition, this was the first time Richard had ever been able to do it without incident. Because his Flexibility Chart was on top of his desk and his teacher was prepared to place a sticker on it, Richard was able to see an immediate reward for his actions. Richard continued to cry or withdraw two to three days a week, but over the course of a month such behavior was reduced to once a week, until he was able to transition smoothly from silent reading to math after two months of flexibility training.

Not all instances of flexibility training are so successful. Some students will need frequent rewards as their Flexibility Chart is filled in with stickers, perhaps receiving a reward for each row that is completed. Bonus stickers may be added to the chart when the student demonstrates flexibility in situations other than the one written on the back of the chart. For example, Richard received a bonus sticker for giving another student a puzzle he himself had chosen to do, instead selecting to do a different activity rather than get upset. This helps reinforce flexible thinking and actions and motivates the student to generalize the behavior.

Students who do not learn to be flexible have a difficult time, not only at school but at home and in community settings. They do not understand the concept of sharing or working as a team. They often find it difficult, if not impossible, to follow directions; and, they are frequently at odds with their peers. Sometimes, teachers and parents try to make the situation less upsetting by allowing the child to do whatever she wishes just to avoid a meltdown or a clash between children. This is tempting, but it is not in the student's best interest (*if* the child is stable) as it reinforces the student's egocentric view of the world and egocentric manner of acting.

Adjusting to changes within the school day, such as transitioning from one task to another, is difficult for many students with AS, as seen in the example with Richard. Although Richard is familiar with the routine and knows when it is time to transition, he finds it frustrating because it is not what he has in mind. As previously stated, individuals with AS are rigid thinkers and have trouble changing their mind-set. Thus, they have trouble starting and stopping activities and, at times, complying with rules. Although this can be difficult to manage, it pales in comparison to managing situations where the student with AS is confronted with an unexpected change. In preparing for such instances, it is important to have visuals like Change in Routine Cards, Option Cards, and Emergency Cards (see Chapter Three) and a home base available. It is also imperative to have an adult responsible for the student who is having difficulty coping with unexpected change and begins to tantrum, rage, or have a meltdown. This person can be a paraprofessional, inclusion facilitator, social worker, or any other adult trained to work with the student during difficult moments.

One way to help the student learn to cope with unexpected change is to rehearse events that might occur unexpectedly like fire drills, a teacher becoming ill and leaving school, or a power outage. Meet privately with the student, and write or provide pictures of these events. Then role-play with the student by modeling how to react. When the actual event does occur, it is also important to provide visuals.

> **Adjusting to changes within the school day is difficult for many students with AS.**

When you systematically teach the child to adjust to change, expect resistance at first, but the rewards can be tremendous. Over time, the student learns the benefits of complying with rules, adjusting to change, and dealing appropriately with the unexpected as he gains control over his emotions and impulsiveness. Students who learn to be flexible have a much greater chance of adjusting to school and to life in general. Imagine how much trouble the student will have as he reaches adulthood if he never learns to deal with change and unexpected events! How will he be able to cope with new demands at work or unexpected changes in personnel? Minor car trouble may be too difficult to handle, or the daily demands of taking care of himself and his home may be impossible to manage. Flexibility training and rehearsal of unexpected events help children with AS learn how to adjust to change and lead happy, independent lives.

Students who learn to be flexible have a much greater chance of adjusting to school and to life in general.

Attending Assemblies

Loud or unexpected noises, bright lights, certain frequencies, and crowds can be very distressing for students with AS. Therefore, plan accordingly for assemblies. Allow students with AS to sit where they are most comfortable. Some are capable of sitting with their classes for the entire assembly; some like to sit with the teacher or by the door; yet others prefer not to attend at all. If the student with AS is extremely anxious at assemblies, it causes a problem for both the student herself and the other students. Provide options, be flexible, and consider what is in the student's best interest.

Having a Substitue Teacher

There are several considerations to make when a substitute teacher is going to take over the class. First, leave the substitute an information sheet about your students with special needs (see Table 5.1). Also provide the substitute teacher copies of the student's Emergency Card and Option Cards.

TABLE 5.1
Student Information for Substitute Teachers

One of my students, _____, has a neurobiological condition known as Asperger Syndrome (AS). As a result, certain things in the school setting are difficult for this student. Students with AS typically have trouble in social situations and when their routine is changed. They also have trouble with handwriting, making eye contact, and with loud sounds like a fire drill.

The following is a list of situations that might be difficult for this student to handle:

The following is a list of behaviors the student might exhibit when feeling overwhelmed or under stress:

The following is a list of strategies you can use when you see the student exhibiting these behaviors:

Anxiety is a **serious** problem for children with AS, and it can escalate rapidly. If you notice this student doing any of the following: _____ _____, immediately ask _____ in room number _____ to help you. Please do **not** try to handle it on your own because there are specific methods for handling this type of problem.

Because students with AS have difficulty when an unexpected change occurs, give advance notice – whether the night before or the morning the substitute teacher is to arrive. Notice can be given by the teacher, the school secretary or some other individual chosen by the teacher. At the beginning of the school year, set up a system for giving notice. A call home from the teacher or other staff member, a discussion with the student the day before the substitute comes, or a note to the parents are some of the ways to handle this more smoothly. It is also a good idea to have a familiar support person visit the room periodically during the teacher's absence. This person can offer reassurance and assistance, if needed. However, some students become so anxious when their teacher is absent that alternative plans must be made. For example, Jon, a fifth-grader, spends the day in the resource room when his homeroom teacher is absent. Jon knows the routine of the resource room, has a good relationship with the resource room teacher, and is less anxious in there than he would be in his regular classroom with a substitute.

When one of the special teachers (music, art, gym) has a substitute, be sure to let the student with AS know in advance. Reassure her that you will still be around if she needs you, and tell her when the special teacher is due back at school. This extra effort on your part will likely help prevent some of the difficult behaviors that can arise when the student with AS is put in an unfamiliar situation.

Exiting During a Fire Drill

Fire drills can be especially frightening to the student with AS, and the noise, surprise, and crowded halls can trigger any number of behaviors. If possible, obtain permission to either inform the student of the upcoming alarm or have the student removed from the room just prior to the drill and escorted out of the building with a familiar staff member. In the event of a real emergency, have a plan for an extra staff member to accompany your class if the student needs assistance. An Emergency Card (see Figure 3.11) can be used to help direct the student if she becomes too anxious to remember what to do. Remember, when anxiety is high, the student has difficulty comprehending verbal instructions and may not be able to do what she has rehearsed.

The student's reaction will depend on a number of variables: sensitivity to loud sounds, ability to adjust to quick changes and surprises, tolerance of crowds and movement, and general temperament for the day. Once you become familiar with the student, you will be able to make a plan for fire drills, enabling the student to react appropriately and safely during an emergency.

Going on a Field Trip

Another source of fear and anxiety for the student with AS is the field trip. When planning for excursions, consider the student's need for routine and sameness, social difficulties, and particular sensory sensitivities. Discuss the field trip with the parents and student, plan for surprises, and arrange for supervision to help make the experience enjoyable for all. A Field Trip Plan such as the one in Table 5.2 can help prepare the student for a field trip.

TABLE 5.2
Field Trip Plan

Field Trip Plan for: _____

To: _____

On: _____ Time: _____

Things I will see: Things I will do:

_____   _____

_____   _____

_____   _____

_____   _____

If I need help, I will: _____

_____

_____

Before Marianna goes on a field trip, her teacher talks to her in private and helps her complete a Field Trip Plan. Marianna experiences very high anxiety when she goes to an unfamiliar place, and this type of preparation helps her relax and enjoy the trip. She likes to know how long the ride is, what she will see and do, and where the bathrooms are. She also likes to know if she can have a drink if she becomes thirsty and if the teacher or a parent volunteer will be the chaperone for her group. Marianna's teacher discusses all of this with her a few days prior to the trip and sends a copy of the Field Trip Plan home so her mother can review everything with her the night before the trip. This type of support helps students with AS prepare for a new and unfamiliar experience.

Arriving Home

Students with AS typically need more wind-down time than others. Overburdening them with homework will affect not only their performance on the homework assignment, but also their behavior at home. If you notice that a student is very anxious at school, consider limiting the amount of homework you assign that night. If the demands of the day are too high, some students will melt down once they get home and never calm down until they go to sleep.

Students with AS typically need more wind-down time than others.

Anxiety-provoking situations and events are numerous within a student's day, posing challenges for both teachers and school staff. The suggestions offered in this section have proven successful for many students with AS. However, some students continue to have problems. Anxiety can result in tantrums, rage, and meltdowns (Myles & Southwick, 1999), and school staff must be prepared to deal with this. Prevention, rather than intervention, should be the rule for students who tantrum, rage, or have a meltdown at school. In the following section, we will discuss difficult moments and the rage cycle (Myles & Southwick, 1999) along with suggestions for how to best manage these situations.

Difficult Moments

School is a major source of stress for children with AS, and when under stress many of them are unable to control their behaviors and emotions (Myles & Southwick, 1999). Some openly demonstrate that they are upset by their words and actions; others internalize their feelings. Regardless, a tantrum, rage, or meltdown may ensue. It is important to be familiar with the rage cycle (Myles & Southwick, 1999) and have a plan in place for dealing with difficult moments.

In order to successfully help students who exhibit tantrums, rage, or meltdowns (TRMs), it is important to first *recognize the signs* of anxiety. Next, the staff must have a list of triggers so everyone will *be prepared* to help the student once his anxiety level has risen. If the student has begun to rage, tantrum, or meltdown, those involved must remember to *maintain control* as help is given to the student. Finally, they must *follow up* the event with a discussion after the student has calmed down (see Myles & Southwick, 1999, for a thorough discussion of this important topic).

In dealing with a difficult moment, you need to be able to recognize the signs of anxiety students may display during the initial stage of a TRM (see Myles & Southwick, 1999). The signs vary from student to student, but may include hand-biting, rocking, flapping arms or hands, putting the head down, spinning, tapping fingers, clearing throat or difficulty processing verbal language. When a difficult moment occurs, use Option Cards and hand signals to communicate with the student, as well as a calm and reassuring voice. Anger and scorn only serve to escalate the situation.

Although some teachers and school staff report that TRMs occur without warning, Myles and Southwick (1999) argue otherwise. They recommend that teachers become familiar with the rage cycle in an effort to learn the signs indicating that a TRM is impending. When the student begins to show signs of distress, intervention is needed immediately because this is the stage when the student can become very anxious and out of control. If handled appropriately and calmly, the fire can be put out before it becomes a raging blaze. Often, the appropriate preventive measures, such as priming and using visuals, will stop the cycle from occurring.

When the rage cycle begins, the first stage is a *rumbling stage* where the student exhibits anxious or repetitive precursor behaviors like finger-biting, chewing on clothing, grimacing, tense muscles, withdraw, argue, or other behaviors they use when feeling anxious or frustrated (Myles & Southwick, 1999). The adult should not become part of a power struggle at this point, but use one of the following nonpunitive strategies suggested in *Asperger Syndrome and Difficult Moments: Practical Solutions for Tantrums, Rage, and Meltdowns* (Myles & Southwick, 1999) to calm the student and stop the cycle:

Antiseptic bouncing – Remove the student from the situation or environment without reprimand by sending him on an errand, going for a drink, or other similar activity/task.

Proximity control – Circulate through the classroom and stand next to the student. This method worked well for Mitchell, a fifth-grader with AS. Whenever his teacher noticed that he was rocking, she would stand next to his desk and continue the lesson from there. The teacher's proximity helped Mitchell regain control.

Signal interference – Use a signal such as a hand signal or finger snap to indicate to the student that she is beginning to engage in a precursor behavior.

Touch control – Touch the student's foot, for example, to bring attention to the behavior to stop it from occurring, such as foot tapping or kicking.

Defusing tension through humor – Use a joke or humorous remark to defuse a potentially tense or eruptive moment for either the student or the class. Be certain the student with AS does not perceive himself as the target of the joke.

Support from routine – Use a visual schedule and refer to it to provide a sense of predictability for the student.

Interest boosting – Show interest in the student and her hobbies by making her aware that you know what they are or by presenting a lesson or doing an activity centered around her special interest.

Redirecting – Help the student focus on something other than what is making him anxious. For example, give him a different activity than the one the rest of the class is doing.

Home base – Use the home base (social worker's office, resource room, and other private locations) as a place where the student can go when he cannot tolerate working in the classroom any longer. He can take his assignments to the home base and continue to work on them in a less stressful environment.

Acknowledging student difficulties – Recognize the student's difficulty and tell him a rule. Do not engage in a power struggle, but use a calm and firm voice, stand close, but do not demonstrate any threatening behaviors like pointing or raising your voice. This strategy is helpful in a situation where a student is having a difficult time sharing with others, for example. Acknowledge that it is difficult to stop playing with a toy when you really like it and then tell the student, "Meaghan, everyone in the classroom must share the toys" (RULE). Be certain to say the student's name so she knows you are talking to her specifically.

Just walk and don't talk – Walk with the student, as long as he is not a "runner," and allow him to say whatever he pleases as this will help him to calm down. Listen without reacting or engaging in a conversation and do not become confrontational.

For some children with AS, physical exercise helps overcome a difficult moment. Jumping on a mini-tramp or running around the the gym or blacktop are good options for some. Running up and down a flight of stairs a few times helps my son calm down. For other children, rolling up or getting under a blanket, sleeping bag, or beanbag chair is relaxing.

Myles and Southwick (1999) emphasize that it is imperative to know the student well, as certain strategies may help calm the student while others will escalate a problem behavior. For example, redirecting and interest-boosting work well for Marianna, but she does not like to be touched, especially when her anxiety level is high. Attempting to touch Marianna would send her right into a rage. Therefore, her teacher avoids touch control when trying to calm her, relying instead on strategies that have been found effective for her.

When a problem behavior has escalated, the student becomes more difficult to manage. This is when the student is out of control and his reasoning ability is gone! If the child has begun a TRM,

153

Myles and Southwick recommend getting him to a predetermined, safe location. This may be a room where there is nothing he can destroy or use to injure himself or others, or it may be the place where the incident occurred. In the latter case, remove items that may be in his way and have someone escort the rest of the class out of the room. Whatever the location, it must be a place where the student can calm down and regain control and dignity.

Do NOT discuss anything with the student until AFTER he has calmed down and regained composure.

Immediately following the rage stage is the *recovery stage* (Myles & Southwick, 1999). During this time, some students cannot remember what happened, may be in denial of any inappropriate behavior, have extreme feelings of guilt and sadness, and/or be exhausted. This is not the time to "teach the student a lesson" or punish him. Wait for a private time when the student is in a state of mind where you can calmly discuss strategies for controlling his emotions such as physical exercise or going to the home base.

Another important step in preparing for and managing difficult moments is *create a crisis plan* (Myles & Southwick, 1999). Just as you would prepare for a fire by having fire drills, prepare both the students and the staff for a crisis involving rage. The following Student Crisis Plan Sheet and acompanying Crisis Report Form are useful for planning and implementing strategies for dealing with rage outbursts at school.

The Student Crisis Plan Sheet shown in Figure 5.2 outlines the antecedents to problem behaviors, the student's typical behaviors at each stage of the rage cycle as well as interventions needed at each stage. As suggested by Myles and Southwick, everyone should use the same plan to ensure consistency and predictability for the student. They also recommend that the Crisis Report Form (see Figure 5.3) be used whenever a student exhibits behaviors that are part of the rage cycle. As illustrated, this form is used to document the student's behavior, interventions implemented, and the effectiveness of the measures taken to assist the student during the crisis. Furthermore, it can be used as a basis for comparing effective interventions.

Student Crisis Plan Sheet

Student Name _____   Student Age/Grade _____

Teacher Name _____   Date of Plan _____

ENVIRONMENTAL/PERSONNEL CONSIDERATIONS

1. Describe how you can obtain assistance when it is needed _____
   _____
   _____

2. At which stage should outside assistance be sought?

   _____ rumbling   _____ rage   _____ recovery

3. Which school personnel are available to provide assistance?

   _____ principal   _____ school psychologist   _____ paraprofessional
   _____ social worker   _____ counselor
   _____ other (please specify) _____
   _____ other (please specify) _____

4. Where should child(ren) exit to? (specify room or school) _____

5. At what stage should the plan be used by others in the classroom?

   _____ rumbling   _____ rage   _____ recovery

6. Are there any extenuating circumstances that others should know about this student (i.e., medications, related medical conditions, home situation)?

7. Who should be notified of the incident? _____

8. How should the incident be documented? _____

Figure 5.2. Student crisis plan sheet.

From *Asperger Syndrome and Difficult Moments: Practical Solutions for Tantrums, Rage and Meltdowns* (pp. 51-53), by B.S. Myles & J. Southwick, 1999. Shawnee Mission, KS: AAPC. Reprinted with permission.

RUMBLING STAGE

1. What environmental factors/activities or antecedents lead to "rumbling" behaviors?

_____ unplanned change _____ difficult assignment _____ crowds
_____ teacher criticism _____ transitions _____ conflict with classmate
_____ other (please describe) _____

2. What behaviors does the student exhibit during the rumbling stage?

_____ bites nails _____ tenses muscles _____ stares
_____ taunts others _____ refuses to work _____ fidgets
_____ other (please describe) _____
_____ other (please describe) _____

3. Does the student mention any of the following complaints or illness?

_____ stomachache _____ headache _____ not applicable
_____ other (please describe) _____

4. Should the student be sent to the nurse if there is a complaint of illness?

_____ yes _____ no

5. How long does the rumbling stage last before it progresses to the next stage?

_____

6. What interventions should be used at this stage?

_____ antiseptic bouncing _____ proximity control _____ touch control
_____ "just walk and don't talk" _____ home base _____ redirecting
_____ other (please specify) _____
_____
_____ other (please specify) _____
_____

Figure 5.2. Continued

RAGE STAGE

1. What behaviors does the student exhibit during the rage stage?

_____ student verbally lashes out at teacher
_____ student verbally lashes out at students
_____ student threatens to hit teacher
_____ student threatens to hit students
_____ student destroys materials
_____ student attempts to leave classroom
_____ student withdraws from teacher
_____ student hurts self
_____ other (please specify) _____
_____ other (please specify) _____

2. What teacher interventions should be used during this stage?

_____ physically move child to safe room
_____ prompt child to move to safe room
_____ remove others from the classroom
_____ redirect student
_____ other (please specify) _____
_____ other (please specify) _____

3. What is the role of others in the child's environment during the rage stage?
_____
_____
_____

RECOVERY STAGE

1. What behaviors does the student exhibit during the recovery stage without intervention?

_____ sullenness
_____ withdrawal into fantasy
_____ denial
_____ "typical" student behavior
_____ other (please describe) _____
_____ other (please describe) _____

2. What supportive techniques should be used during this stage? _____
_____
_____

3. What interventions should be used at a later time to assist the student in gaining more self-control? _____
_____
_____

Figure 5.2. Continued

Crisis Report Form

Student Name _____

Teacher Name _____

Setting _____ Date _____

Antecedent Events _____

Rumbling Stage

Student Behavior _____

_____

Teacher Interventions _____

_____

Rage Stage

Student Behavior _____

_____

Teacher Interventions _____

_____

Recovery Stage

Student Behavior _____

_____

Teacher Interventions _____

_____

Other Considerations

_____

_____

Figure 5.3. Crisis report form.

From *Asperger Syndrome and Difficult Moments: Practical Solutions for Tantrums, Rage and Meltdowns* (p. 54), by B.S. Myles & J. Southwick, 1999. Shawnee Mission, KS: AAPC. Reprinted with permission.

Many instances of tantrums, rage, or meltdowns at school are caused by difficulties in social situations. Efforts should be made to help students with AS learn to navigate successfully through stressful social situations. In the next section, the importance of play and how it helps children develop social skills is explained. Because most children with AS do not play like their neurotypical peers, they often do not develop social skills through play, and must be systematically taught specific social skills.

The Importance of Play

Play serves a universal role in helping children develop social skills, explore their environment, make discoveries about the world, and acquire language (Wolfberg, 1999, 2002). Preschools and kindergartens focus on play as a means of developing these skills. Neurotypical students thrive in these environments and relatively quickly learn such communication and social skills as negotiating, persuading, adapting, and tolerating. However, children

Play serves a universal role in helping children develop social skills.

with AS do not acquire social skills in the same way or at the same time as their peers. When in preschool and kindergarten, they often avoid social interactions, disrupt play, and/or engage in injurious behaviors or self-stimulatory activities.

When neurotypical students enter the primary grades, assistance and facilitation with play gradually stops, as they acquire the necessary social skills and language competence to interact independently with their peers. However, students with AS need a chance to catch up socially and emotionally before play opportunities with assistance are discontinued. If a child with a physical disability needs her wheelchair to play a game with the other children, it is provided without a question. Similarly, if a child with a pervasive developmental disorder such as AS needs support and guidance in order to play a game with her peers, it should be provided.

Sample Questions for Informal Play Evaluation

1. How does the child communicate? Describe the child's expressive language when in a natural play setting. For example, *She does not use words to communicate her wishes. When she wants something, she grabs it from another child or cries.*

2. Identify purposes of communication such as requests, offering assistance, acceptance, refusal, joint attention, sharing information, and seeking information. Example of a request: *He wanted a book that another child was reading so he told the child to let go in a very loud voice.*

3. Describe the way in which the child responds when a peer speaks to him. For example, *When asked to share a toy, she threw the toy at the child asking for it.*

4. Describe the child's use of nonverbal expression. Consider eye contact, body language, and use of personal space.

5. Describe the child's understanding of nonverbal communication. Identify situations in which the child correctly interpreted nonverbal communication and situations where she misinterpreted it or did not interpret it at all.

6. Identify types of initiations the child attempts. For example, using another child's name to engage her in an activity or any other action, such as bumping a child or running in circles around other children, to get their attention. Describe both the behavior and the language of the student you are observing as well as that of the other children involved.

7. Identify the stage of development: *manipulative, functional,* or *symbolic.* For example, does the child use cups to pretend she is having a tea party or does she use them as supports to build a bridge? Or does she use a block and pretend it is a cup while she is having a tea party?

8. Identify level of play: *solitary* (plays alone), *observing* (watches other children play), *parallel* (plays next to, but not with other children), *joint activity* (plays the same game or participates in the same activity as other children), *collaboration* (actively works with another child or children to create or construct an object, a game, an activity, or a plan).

9. Identify preferences in activities, objects, and peers.

10. Compare number of appropriate actions, interactions, and behaviors to inappropriate actions, interactions, and behaviors. Keep a tally for a 15- to 20-minute period over several days in various settings. Furthermore, look for patterns in behavior such as *Most inappropriate behaviors took place when there were more than four children in the room* or *He interacted appropriately with his peers when they were playing with trucks.*

Figure 5.4. Sample questions for informal play evaluation.

Evaluating Play

Before assisting students with AS during play, the teacher and therapists must evaluate the student's linguistic competence, developmental level of play activities, and level and type of interactions. An informal play evaluation can be used to give general information about your student with AS prior to creating social skills goals. Figure 5.4 contains examples of questions to be considered when conducting an informal play evaluation. The questions are meant to serve only as a guide. It is recommended that a thorough evaluation be completed by a diagnostician, psychologist, or social worker and that tools such as *The Developmental Play Assessment Instrument* (Lifter, 2000), *The Play Task Analysis, Play Interest Survey* (Quill, 2000), or *Play Evaluation Guide* (Wolfberg, 2002) be used to further evaluate the student.

Using Play to Develop Social Skills

Based upon the results of the play evaluation, determine the amount and types of intervention and support the student will need. To do so, meet with all support staff and the parents to review evaluations of the student at play and create IEP goals that address the student's needs in this area. For example, the team may determine that the student needs five hours per week of direct instruction and practice in social skills. The team also identifies specific skills to be targeted, such as *Asks a peer to join him in an activity*. The following is a list of some of the target behaviors to consider when planning a social skills program for students with AS (see Baker, 2003, for additional social skills).

- Attempts to participate
- Asks others to join him/her in an activity
- Looks at others when playing with them
- Uses names of children to get their attention
- Uses words to communicate wants/dislikes/needs
- Shares toys/objects
- Offers assistance appropriately
- Accepts/refuses assistance appropriately
- Seeks help appropriately

- Uses body language to communicate
- Respects personal space of others
- Accurately interprets nonverbal communication
- Observes others to learn new activities, game rules, procedures
- Works cooperatively with peer(s) to complete an activity or play a game
- Initiates a conversation
- Responds to nonverbal solicitations to play

After the target skills have been determined, identify the team members who will be responsible for (a) implementing the program, (b) monitoring the student's progress, and (c) determining the frequency of assessment of progress.

There are many things to consider when planning social skills training for students with AS. First, provide a predictable environment, whether it is the classroom or the therapist's office. Be sure to provide a schedule of activities/ events, use visuals, and prepare the students as best as possible for any anticipated or planned changes. Because these children have difficulty dealing with change, consistency and familiarity will help them experience success as they work toward obtaining new skills.

Unstructured play times

When using unstructured play time to teach social skills, define the play space with clear boundaries like an area rug, moveable book shelves, toy bins, or tables. In addition, organize play materials on a shelf or in a bin where they are easy to locate, and make sure a sufficient number of play choices are available without overloading the student.

To begin social skills instruction during unstructured play time, the student is encouraged to explore the area and play with the toys. At this stage, only the adult facilitator and the child are in the room. The adult makes comments and asks questions about what the student is doing, modeling the target skills identified for the student. For instance, if you are modeling the skill of seeking help appropriately, you would say, "Chris, will you help me open this box?" When you notice the student needs help with something, you script him by saying, "It looks like you need help with that. Say, 'Ms. Moore, will you help me put this train on the track?'" Thus, the facilitator is providing direct instruction and modeling social skills.

After the child has had experience playing with the adult facilitator, it is time to bring a peer into the play session. The role of the adult facilitator now ranges from periphery observer to coach. When facilitating play, the adult often must tell the student what to do (*coaching*) such as, "Give the ball to Mikey. He is asking you for the ball." Likewise, you will have to give the student lines (*scripting*) like, "Say, I want the ball now." As you help the child in the play interaction, keep the target skills in mind, focusing on only one or two skills to work on each session.

After the student has developed some proficiency at interacting with one peer, introduce more children to the play session. Three or four children dramatically change the dynamics of the interactions, so be prepared to work on previously learned social skills since the student may regress when he feels anxious, which often occurs when there are several children in the room. If the student is not successful playing with a group of children, you may have to introduce new group members slowly, adding only one at a time and providing constant support by coaching and scripting the student throughout the entire session. Adult intervention is the key to achieving success for these students. Be patient. It may take several months for the student to learn how to interact with his peers during a play session.

> **It may take several months for the student to learn how to interact with his peers during a play session.**

Social Skills Instruction

Besides using unstructured play sessions to develop social skills, students with AS often benefit from structured lessons. This may be accomplished in a 1:1 setting, with their peers, or in multi-age groups. Peer groups may include four to five students with or without special needs; multi-age groups usually consist of one or two students who have special needs within a group of four or five students.

The teacher's or therapist's role is to act as a guide and interpreter as the student with AS begins to interact with peers. Asking questions, commenting, offering suggestions, and demonstrating are some of the methods used to assist a student during social skills instructions. Remember, the adult facilitator's assistance is vital to the success of the training so be prepared to do a great deal of talking, not just observing.

Children with AS may need direct instruction in the use of *social language* because, as discussed in Chapter Two, they have trouble understanding the pragmatics of language. Specifically, they do not recognize that the way in which they speak has an impact on the listener, and they do not understand the subtleties of language or the cultural uses of polite language. Simply stated, they often speak without regard for others' thoughts, feelings, or beliefs. Teaching these children how to use social language will help improve their communication skills and social interactions with peers and school staff.

I Can Say (Rules for Social Language)

Since children with AS are frequently rule-driven, using a set of rules for speaking to others, such as those used in the *I Can Say* strategy, will help them learn to use appropriate social language and experience success in their interactions. This strategy teaches appropriate social language by focusing on eight social skills and can be used with students in elementary school, even emergent readers, in 1:1 social skills training sessions or with a small group of three to four students with similar needs. Table 5.3 lists the target social skills and the *I Can Say* social language rules.

Before you begin the training sessions, write each of the eight social skills on index cards so you have one per card. For emergent readers, glue or draw a picture on the index card to demonstrate the skill, such as a picture of a girl handing a boy a toy to depict the first social skill. On the back of the card, write *I Can Say* at the top and under it, write the social language rule for that skill. Keep the cards together for each student by punching a hole in the top left corner of each card and putting them on a key ring each time a new one is given.

TABLE 5.3
I Can Say Target Skills and Social Language Rules

1. Accept/reject an object or an invitation.
To accept something, *I can say*, "Yes, thank you."
To reject something, *I can say*, "No, thank you."

2. Ask a friend to play
When I want to play with someone, *I can say*, "Would you like to play with me?" or *I can say*, "Would you like to see my toy?"

3. Join a game
When I want to join a game, *I can say*, "May I play with you?"

4. Deal with rejection from an individual
When someone doesn't want to play with me, *I can say*, "Okay," and walk away. I can also ask another person to play or play alone.

5. Deal with rejection from group
When a group of children don't want me to play with them, *I can say*, "Okay," and walk away.

6. Request assistance
If I need help, *I can say*, "I need help, please."

7. Offer assistance
When I think someone needs my help, *I can say*, "May I help you with that?" or *I can say*, "Would you like some help?"

8. Express Opinions
When I want to tell someone that I like something, *I can say*, "I like that." When I want to tell someone that I don't like something, *I can say*, "I don't like that," or "It's okay to have different opinions. I don't like that."

Front of card

I Can Say:
"Yes, thank you."

Back of card

When meeting with the student (or group of students), present one social skill and rule at a time. This is important, as presenting more than one skill/rule per session may lead to confusion and anxiety. Role-play the social skill with the student, scripting him if necessary with the *I Can Say* lines for each skill. Repeat this activity for each of the eight social skills, presenting one skill at a time, and reviewing a skill over a couple of sessions when the student is having difficulty remembering the social language rule. For students having difficulty remembering what to say for each skill, visual aids such as puppets, drawings, and photos may be used.

After the student has learned what to say, he will need help identifying situations in which the rules apply. Reward attempts at following the rules during role-play. For example, after being prompted, if the student asks if you need assistance and accepts your reply, give him a point or sticker as a reward. As the student begins to follow the social rules spontaneously, be sure to reward him again. This will help reinforce the behavior and lock it into his memory because it is linked to a positive experience.

Another important step in using this strategy is to point out what the student *cannot* say or do. The facilitator may have to identify the student's inappropriate language or actions for him, because students with AS are often unaware of or unable to identify their own unacceptable behavior. For example, Valerie says, "I think you are stupid!" when peers tell her they do not want to play with her. In this instance, the facilitator would tell Valerie that she cannot say, "I think you are stupid!" because those words are inappropriate and hurt people's feelings. Then, on the back of her *I Can Say* card for "Deals with Rejection from an Individual," write: I CANNOT say, "I think you are stupid!" Now the card has a target social skill on one side and what the student can say and cannot say or do on the back.

This strategy teaches the student with AS what to say and how to act in specific social situations. Students with AS often need to be told what they can and cannot say or do because they do not realize that some of the things they say and do are inappropriate or impolite.

> **Students with AS often need to be told what they can and cannot say or do.**

The strategy worked very well for Marianna. She brought in a favorite key ring to hold her cards. The words "I Can Say" on the back of the card were written in green and "I Cannot" in red. Using color helped Marianna remember what to say or do. When Marianna went to the park, she took her key ring of *I Can Say* cards with her, and even though she kept the cards in her pocket most of the time, she did take them out once in a while to help her remember what to say. More important, Marianna and her teacher reviewed the cards before she went to the park. Reviewing the *I Can Say* index cards helps the student with AS remember how to act.

It is a good idea to provide a copy of the student's *I Can Say* cards to all of his teachers and therapists so they know the target skills being taught and the way in which they are being taught. Likewise, give a copy of the cards to the student's parents so they can help reinforce the social language rules in situations outside of school. The team effort will pay off; it may take a few months, but the proficiency the student will gain and the satisfaction he will feel will do wonders for his self-esteem and confidence in social situations.

Social Language Groups (co-authored by Sally Bligh, CCC-SLP)

Social Language Groups (SLGs), originated by speech-language pathologist Sally Bligh, is a method for teaching social interaction skills to children with impaired or delayed communication and social development in school and therapy settings, as well as in the home. SLG can be used to teach reciprocal peer communication through the use of techniques such as:

Scripting: This is used when the child does not know what to say in the social situation and the adult gives the child the exact words to say, just like in a play when the prompter provides the lines the actor cannot recall.

Game playing: This technique is used to encourage verbal interchange. Games and activities are carefully selected and must require participants to interact.

Exploring special interests: The child's special interest is used to motivate and encourage participation in social interactions.

Positive reinforcement: Concrete, visible rewards such as stickers or points marked on a piece of paper are used to reinforce the desired social behavior. This is highly effective because of the child's strong desire to be perfect and avoid errors.

Modeling: The facilitator demonstrates the appropriate behavior as the group members observe.

Role-playing: Having the child practice being in different social situations is a useful way of rehearsing new skills. Adding videotaping increases the effectiveness because the child can later view himself to see if what he did was actually what he had intended to do.

In preparing to conduct SLGs, consider the following four components:

- child's communication level
- number of children in each group
- activities/games that will be used
- reward system

We will briefly look at each of these factors below.

Communication level

Before children are assigned to a group, their communication level must be evaluated. This can be done by observing them during a recess period or free-choice activity to identify the communication level that best describes their behaviors and communication skills (see below). Although some children may exhibit behaviors and communication skills described in a couple of levels, determine which behaviors and communication skills *are most frequently occurring* in order to determine their communication level. These levels, as identified by Sally Bligh, are as follows:

1. *No verbal exchange.* Children at this level know how to talk but do not know what to say to their peers. Often they play alone, even when surrounded by other children who are playing something they really enjoy.

2. *Needs to control and win.* At this level, the child is beginning to talk to other children. She may use rehearsed social phrases such as "Do you want to play with me" but she then tells the children what she wants them to do. In other words, she needs to control, be in charge, and win. She has meltdowns or becomes angry when she is not in control or is losing. Others find it difficult to play with a child on this level.

3. *Gives commands.* Children on this level do not engage in conversations but give commands and make comments that do not invite a response. For example, while playing a game, children with AS often give commands to the other children, telling them where to sit, how to play, etc. Sometimes they even make up their own rules. In other words, they try to dominate by giving orders to everyone.

4. *Monologues.* Children on this level talk to their peers, but their communicative efforts are not yet reciprocal. They talk on and on about a topic of interest to them, ignoring the reactions and responses of their listeners.

5. *Changes the subject.* At this level, the children are beginning to communicate with each other, but they often change the subject abruptly while conversing, thereby breaking the flow of the communication and confusing the listener. It is difficult for children with AS to maintain their focus on a topic if they are interested in talking about something else. For example, while a group of children are discussing video games, the student with AS may begin talking about her favorite interest, hummingbirds. She changes the subject without a transition and leaves the other children confused and disinterested.

Grouping

While Social Language Groups may be formed in a number of different ways, it is best to start with a group of children who communicate on approximately the same level. Group size should not exceed five members, and the group meeting place should be free from distractions and of a size that can comfortably accommodate the group. SLGs can be run by a speech-language pathologist, social worker, or anyone interested in and committed to learning the methods for conducting the group sessions.

Group size should not exceed five members.

Activities

Once the groups have been formed, appropriate activities must be selected, including activities that will encourage the children to play with each other (see Table 5.4). When selecting games, be sure to consider the children's social and emotional levels. Games of chance are much more stressful than games requiring skill. Consistency in rules and expectations will help reduce the stress of game playing. Some games incorporate both chance and skill, making them the most difficult for children with AS.

Because children with AS tend to be perfectionistic, rigid thinkers, and inflexible, game playing may also be very stressful for the group facilitator. The facilitator must be prepared to handle arguments, building anxiety, meltdowns, and the like. If necessary, a given activity may be stopped and another started. Sometimes, the facilitator may "bend" the rules by changing cards or moving pieces inconspicuously to change the course of the game. Since the goal is to teach reciprocal peer communication, the focus on winning needs to be eliminated. Sometimes, the game is intentionally stopped so that no one wins and no one loses, focusing on just the play and the verbal exchanges.

In addition to games, facilitators may want to incorporate the students' special interests (Gagnon, 2001) into group activities. For example, if a couple of the members are interested in a particular cartoon, have them bring in some action figures and comic books to share. The students can take turns sharing their items and engaging in conversations about them. The facilitator can help guide the discussion by interrupting monologues, asking questions, and encouraging other members to participate as she models conversing and rewards the group members' attempts to converse.

Rewards

There are a variety of ways to reward and reinforce behaviors during group sessions. Begin by introducing the Social Language Group rule for the day (see Table 5.4) and give points to members who are CAUGHT FOLLOWING THE RULES. For example, give little tickets that say "I was caught following the rules!" At the end of the session, tally up each member's tickets and record them on a chart. Send a note home to the parents to let them know which rules you practiced and how many tickets their child earned. Offer rewards that will motivate the students as they earn tickets.

Another way to reward the students is to give them points every time they make a comment that invites a response. For example, if a group member asks another member a question such as "Which color do you want?" rather than saying, "I want red!," that member would earn a point because asking someone a question invites a response. Remind the students that comments must relate to the activity they are engaged in. Some children with AS are very adept at figuring out the easiest way to accumulate points and without rules will begin asking question after question about any topic just to earn points.

Communication training

After groups have been formed, activities chosen, and a reward system developed, the facilitator begins to take the students through five levels of communication. It may take months or years to move children through the five levels, and some children may progress at a faster rate than others. Therefore, it is essential to keep grouping flexible. Repeated practice is essential for success. As the students gain an understanding of social rules, and as they learn how to play games, they will begin to interact with their peers.

At each communication level, the children are encouraged to talk to each other. As they attempt to communicate, the facilitator presents a specific rule for the students to learn and uses a particular technique to teach the rule (see Table 5.4).

TABLE 5.4
Social Language Groups

Level One: No verbal exchange

Rule – *Say What I Say*
Technique – Scripting, positive reinforcement
Suggested Activities/Games – Use activities and toys with no winning or losing involved, such as bubbles, marble tower, trains, dinosaurs, cars, tea sets, puppets

Level Two: Needs to win and control

Rule – *Sometimes I Win And Sometimes I Lose*
Techniques – Scripting, game playing, modeling, positive reinforcement
Suggested Activities – Use simple turn-taking games like *Go Fish, Memory, T-Rex Rules*™, *ABSeas*™, *Guess Who*™, *Hi Ho! Cherry-O*™, *Fishin' Fun*™, *Come Play With Me*™, *Topple*™, *Mouse Trap*™, *Things In My House*™, *Don't Spill The Beans, Uno*™, and simple board games like *Splat*™, *Leaping Lilypads*™, *Candyland*™, and *Don't Wake Daddy*™

Level Three: Gives commands

Rule – *Talk To Each Other In A Way To Make Friends*
Techniques – Scripting, game playing, modeling, positive reinforcement
Suggested Activities/Games – Use strategy games such as *Trouble*™, *Secret Square Board Game*™, *20 Questions*™, *Chutes and Ladders*™, *Connect Four, Aggrivation*™, and *Pit*™

TABLE 5.4 CONTINUED

Level Four: Monologues

Rule – *Say Two Things Then Ask A Question* '
Techniques – Scripting, game playing, modeling, using special interests, role-playing, positive reinforcement
Suggested Activities/Games – Use complex board games such as *Sorry™, Trivial Pursuit Games, Risk™, Extinction™, Clue™, Parcheesi™*, and *Monopoly.* (These games are more difficult than those used in previous levels, both in strategy and in dealing with "falling back" throughout play such as when you are returned to start or put in jail during the game.) Topics and items of special interest may also be used for this level

Level Five: Changes the subject

Rule – *Only Change The Subject When You Think The Listener Is Ready*
Techniques – Scripting, modeling, using special interests, role-playing, positive reinforcement
Suggested Activities – Use topics and items of special interest as a basis for conversation

The following is a discussion of how to conduct groups at each of the five levels.

Level one: No verbal exchange. At this level, the facilitator's role is to script the dialogue for the children. The rule the children learn is: *Say What I Say,* and the facilitator reminds the children of the rule throughout the session.

The group begins with the children engaging in solitary play. The facilitator then brings the children to the table to create a list of activities to play during the session. The list is written or drawn so it can be referred to throughout the session. The objective is clearly and repeatedly stated: *Talk to each other.* The facilitator uses scripting to help the children with the dialogue. For example, she might provide these words for a child: "Josh, say, *Kevin, do you want to blow bubbles with me?*" Josh repeats, "*Kevin, do you want to blow bubbles with me?*" Next, the facilitator says, "Kevin, say, *Yes, that sounds like fun.*" Kevin repeats, "*Yes, that sounds like fun.*" Then the bubble blowing activity is added to the list. This is repeated for additional activities.

After the list is made, the facilitator engages the children in the activities, again clearly repeating the objective: *Talk to each other.* During the bubble blowing activity, the facilitator would script Josh by saying, "Josh, say, *Kevin, look at this big bubble!*" Josh repeats, "*Kevin, look at this big bubble!*" Then the facilitator tells Kevin, "Kevin, say, *Josh, I see your big bubble!*" Kevin repeats, "*Josh, I see your big bubble!*"

At first, this technique sounds very stilted, but over time the children learn the lines and begin to use them spontaneously. Gradually, they learn how to ask for help, to join in play, to offer assistance, and so on. It is important to use the children's names as illustrated in the example above, as pronouns can be confusing to children with AS. Be sure to get the child's attention by first saying his name and then telling him the exact words to say to the other child. By getting the exact words to say, the child does not have to concentrate on doing something that is difficult. That is, he does not have to generate original language while learning to play with another child.

Throughout the session, the facilitator is teaching the children to take turns by giving them lines to dialogue with each other and by giving them each a turn to blow a bubble. Turn-taking is difficult for many children with AS, so this skill has to be taught. The children have to learn to anticipate their turn, and to wait until it is their turn. Practicing simple turn-taking allows the children to learn the reciprocal communication process.

Level two: Needs to control and win. With this level, the facilitator uses games and gradually increases the level of competition. The rule the children learn is: *Sometimes I Win and Sometimes I Lose*, and the facilitator reminds the children of the rule throughout the game.

To begin, chose a simple turn-taking game or board game for the group to play. Although they involve winning and losing, the games are often quickly completed and then repeated, giving others a chance to win. If a member becomes too agitated to continue playing, suggest it is a time to relax and provide a place for her to cool down. A beanbag chair in the corner of the room is a great cool-down spot. Another idea is to set up large trifold boards as walls around a beanbag chair to create a private spot in the room. Two or three display boards are enough to create the private space. For older children, a desk off to the side with one trifold display board on top will help create a private space where the student can cool down before returning to the group. Some children will need to do something physical when they become agitated. A mini-tramp in the corner of the room or some clay to play with may help a student who needs to do a physical activity in order to calm down.

The facilitator guides the children through the game and scripts them when they need to say things like "It's your turn," "Could you go a bit faster?," or "I need the dice." As the children learn the rules for the game and play it several times, they learn to give up some control and begin to play the game for fun, experiencing both winning and losing. Sometimes, however, the child insists on having her own way such as getting a particular playing piece, following the rules her way, or having to win. In such situations, the facilitator can explain to the group that they will have to choose between arguing or playing. If they choose to play, compromising is taught by having them take turns saying what they will do or not do in order to continue playing. For example, Caitlyn says that she will agree to use the green piece as long as she doesn't have to use red or blue. Michael then agrees to use the red, Paul agrees to use blue, and Jose agrees to use yellow.

But the situation cannot always be resolved with compromise. If one of the children continues to insist on having his way, the facilitator explains to the other children that it is too difficult for the child to compromise right now, so the game will be played his way for a short time and then played the other way. Be specific about how long you will play the game under the child's control. That is, set a timer or write the number of minutes on a piece of a paper and remind the child when the time is about to end so he can prepare himself for ending his control of the game. He is encouraged to consider compromise the next time they play and reminded that playing is more fun than arguing, especially when arguing reduces the number of minutes they will have to play the game.

Another way to teach children with AS to deal with winning and losing is to give them this rule: *Winners Are Losers and Losers Are Winners.* Sally Bligh uses this method frequently to help students begin to focus on playing, not on winning. Sometimes the rules are changed so the prize goes to the loser, and at other times the prize for winning is something undesirable like a silly hat or big plastic glasses. When losing becomes the desired goal, there is a completely different tone to the interaction. Bligh encourages the students to laugh and have fun while playing rather than focusing on winning and losing.

Level three: Gives commands. At this level a game is chosen, as in the previous level. The facilitator continues to script as necessary and rewards comments that invite a response because children on this level frequently give commands without making comments that invite a response. The rule the children learn is: *Talk To Each Other In A Way To Make Friends.*

While the children are playing, reciprocal communication is taught by encouraging them to ask questions of each other about strategies and give compliments rather than orders. For example, during a game of *Sorry*, Brian commands Eric to ignore the instructions on his card. The facilitator scripts Brian to say, "If you follow the instructions on that card, I may not be in the lead. Would you like to chose another card?" If Eric responds by saying no, then Brian is reminded of the rule: *Talk To Each Other In A Way To Make Friends.* Then the facilitator tells Brian to say, "Okay," and reminds him that cooperation is important in game playing and that friends do not like to be given orders. Brian is also reminded that friends may want to end a game if they are constantly given orders.

At this level, the children are learning how to engage in polite conversation while playing a game. They are taught that giving commands does not encourage friends to talk or play with them, and they begin to realize that the way they speak to each other affects the interaction.

Level four: Monologues. Group sessions on this level may or may not involve an activity or game. Instead, the sessions may be divided into two parts, the first half focusing on conversing and the second half on conversing while playing. Whether the group spends the entire session or just half of the period working on conversational skills, the facilitator's role is to provide reminders to the child who is speaking. For example, when a child begins to monologue, the facilitator must interrupt the monologue and remind the child of the rule: *Say Two Things And Then Ask A Question.*

The facilitator begins by introducing a topic for the group to discuss. For example, the facilitator might say, "Bill, ask Morgan what she did this weekend." The facilitator helps the children keep the conversation going and gives points or tickets for any spontaneous comment that invites a response, such as Bill saying, "Morgan, tell me more about the movie you saw on Saturday." Points or tickets are also awarded to children who follow the rule and do not monologue.

Although the children may initially know what to say in response to another child, they usually do not know what to ask next. For example, Bill says, "Morgan, what did you do this weekend?" and she responds by saying, "I saw the new *Star Wars* movie. It was great because it followed the plot from the last movie." It is now Bill's turn to continue the conversation. When left on his own, however, Bill is unable to ask a question in response to Morgan's statement.

> *Children with AS have difficulty formulating questions that are a necessary component of reciprocal conversation.*

Children with AS have difficulty formulating questions that are a necessary component of reciprocal conversation. A neurotypical peer would follow Morgan's statement with a question such as, "Was Darth Vader in this movie?" This question shows that the listener was listening to what was said, was interested in the topic, and responded appropriately, thereby encouraging the speaker to continue the conversation. Children with AS are at a disadvantage in the conversation process because this skill is difficult for them.

To remedy this situation, the facilitator scripts in the questions the children need to ask in order to continue the conversation. In this situation, the facilitator would say, "Bill, ask Laura if Darth Vader was is in the movie." Bill would then say, "Was Darth Vader in this movie?" This question encourages Morgan to continue talking about the movie and keeps the topic of the conversation the same.

If the children do not ask questions of each other, they typically engage in monologuing. The following is an example.

Bill: Laura, what did you do this weekend?

Laura: I saw the new *Star Wars* movie. It was great because it followed the plot from the last movie.

Bill: I don't like *Star Wars*. *Star Trek* is the best! My favorite is *The Next Generation*. It has Captain Piccard. He is the best captain of all the *Star Trek* captains. I can name all of the captains in order: Kirk, Piccard, Bernard, and Janeway. I've seen every episode of the original *Star Trek* series, some of them even two or three times. I have *Star Trek* action figures, and I have 27 *Star Trek* comic books.

Laura: I have 32 *Star Wars* comic books and I have 17 action figures. I have Darth Vader, Luke Sky Walker, Obi-Wan-Konobi, Princess Leah, Queen Amidala, and 12 Storm Troopers. My mom lets me bring them to school in my backpack but she makes me promise to keep them in there.

This is not the way neurotypical children carry on a conversation. They would become bored with the monologuing and give cues to that effect, such as looking away or trying to shift topics. Children with AS do not pick up on body language or attempts to change the topic. They just take turns monologuing. Therefore, they must be specifically taught how to carry on a conversation that includes appropriate questions and statements. The facilitator must stop the monologuing and remind the child of the rule: *Say Two Things And Then Ask A Question.*

In the monologuing example above, the facilitator should stop Bill after he says, "*Star Trek* is the best!," reminding him, "You have just said two things about *Star Trek*. Now ask Morgan a question." Bill may respond by inquiring, "Morgan, do you like *Star*

Trek?" so he can keep the subject on *Star Trek* rather than reverting back to *Star Wars*. Bill may be permitted to ask that question, but the facilitator may have to interrupt Morgan after she answers "No," and begins monologuing about *Star Wars*. The facilitator reminds Morgan to say two things about *Star Wars* and then ask Bill a question.

In addition to reminding the children of the rule *Say Two Things And Then Ask A Question*, the facilitator must teach them to look for clues to see if their listeners are still attending. The facilitator must be very specific, telling the speaker to look at the listener's eyes, shoulders, hands, and so on. It helps to role-play the roles of speaker and listener to point out nonverbal cues that should be attended to while speaking. Children with AS become so absorbed in what they are talking about that they can be completely unaware of what is happening around them.

To teach the rule for this level, practice with the children by first giving them examples of how to say two things, ask a question, and then monologue so they can hear the difference. They will need to be explicitly taught the difference between the two styles of speaking so they can become aware of when they are monologuing. Reward the children when they recognize that they are monologuing and also when they attempt to engage in reciprocal communication. Consistent reinforcement and encouragement will help them learn how to communicate appropriately with their peers.

Level five: Changes the subject. At this level, the children talk to each other about their special interests, and the facilitator instructs the group members on how to get and give feedback. The rule the students learn is: *Only Change The Subject When You Think The Listener Is Ready*. Because it is difficult for children with AS to focus on a topic that is not interesting to them, they often change the subject abruptly to their own interest. When this occurs, the facilitator reminds the speaker of the rule for changing the subject and tells her to check with the group members to see if they are still interested in what she has to say. The facilitator explains why the listeners lose interest and describes how to look for cues that tell the speaker whether her listening audience is interested or not.

The facilitator also explains to the group members how to show that they are interested in what a speaker is saying. Individuals with AS are often not cognizant of the messages they are sending. They may be fiddling with something, looking at the floor, interrupting, or moving around – oblivious that such behavior indicates boredom, confusion, or lack of interest. Consequently, they need to be instructed on how to act when they are interested in what a speaker has

> *Individuals with AS are often not cognizant of the messages they are sending.*

to say. As the children learn how to engage in reciprocal communication, the facilitator's role becomes smaller and smaller until the children are able to carry on a conversation all on their own.

At each level, it is important to role-play and offer incentives and rewards for following the communication rules. It is also effective to offer a grand prize after a student or group has accumulated a certain number of points or tickets. Plan a picnic lunch for the group or inquire if local merchants will donate small gift certificates for the students to earn.

Another way to reward the students is to offer them free-choice time to engage in their favorite activity or special interest. For example, they may earn computer time to play a game or do research on their favorite topic. Some students may want time to talk about their special interests. Others may enjoy staying in at recess to play chess with a classmate. Whatever reward is selected, be certain to use a consistent and predictable reward system so students will know what to expect. There are enough unexpected events at school for them to deal with. The reward system should not be a source of anxiety but a means of encouraging risk-taking and developing self-confidence. As the children's confidence increases, so does their level of communication.

Social Language Groups provide an excellent model for teaching children with AS how to communicate in an environment where they can feel comfortable taking risks and making mistakes as they develop and refine their social skills. They should be an integral part of any social skills training program for students with AS.

Social Stories

Another effective tool for teaching social skills was created by Carol Gray using the strategy she calls Social Stories (Gray, 1995; Gray & Gerand, 1993; Swaggart et al., 1995). Social Stories involve describing a social situation from the student's perspective. The stories may include the student's feelings, her reactions, and the situations in which the social dilemma might occur. They also include options so that the students knows what to do in a given situation.

Alex, a fourth-grader with AS, growls at other children when they ask for a turn with a toy or book he has. To teach Alex appropriate social skills to use, his teacher created the Social Story presented in Table 5.5. This Social Story gave Alex options for the situation and resulted in better interactions between Alex and his peers.

TABLE 5.5
Social Story

Sometimes at school, other children want to play with the toys I have or read the books I am reading. They ask me to share these things because they like them, too.

When they ask me to share, I have many choices. I can tell them to ask the teacher to help us share fairly. I can also say, "Okay" and give them what they want. Another thing I can do is say, "I'm still playing with this right now, but you can have it when I'm done."

When I growl at other children instead of using my choices, the other kids get mad or laugh at me. This makes me feel mad. Sometimes the teacher hears me growl and this makes her upset. Then I get in trouble.

I don't want to get mad or in trouble, so I will use my choices when children want me to share.

Social Stories may be used to teach social skills such as appropriate verbal responses to peers, greetings, avoiding physical contact, and turn-taking. For elementary children, this strategy works best if the stories are kept simple, short, and uncomplicated. When the stories are long narrations of a social situation, students tend to lose interest and fail to gain the rewards this method has to offer.

SOCCSS

In order to help children with social disabilities understand social situations and develop problem-solving skills, Jan Roosa developed the Situation-Options-Consequences-Choices-Strategies-Simulation (SOCCSS) strategy. Briefly, this strategy helps children understand that the choices they make influence the outcome of the situations in which they are involved. The SOCCSS strategy, which can be used with an individual student or a group, may be used after a social problem has occurred or as an instructional strategy to identify and plan for problem situations students may encounter (Myles & Simpson, 2001; Myles & Southwick, 1999). The six steps involved in SOCCSS are as follows:

Situation: With the help of the teacher, the student answers the five "W" questions about the incident (who, what, where, when, why). The student may be reluctant to answer the questions, so prompt, ask questions, and answer the questions for the student, if necessary, until the student is able to do this step independently.

Options: The teacher and student brainstorm a list of things the student could have done differently, and the teacher records them. All behavior options presented by the student are to be accepted without comment. Teachers may have to encourage the student to identify more than one option.

Consequences: Identify the outcome of each option. This is difficult for students with AS, so use role-playing as a prompt to identify the consequence (Myles & Adreon, 2001).

Choices: Prioritize the options with the student. Then ask the student to identify the option he thinks he will be able to do and that will get him what he wants or needs.

Strategies: The student develops a plan of action using the option he has chosen in the previous step. Encourage the student to create this plan independently as this will help make him feel that he is responsible for his choices and actions.

Simulation: Practice the plan of action the student has created. Roosa recommends using a variety of practice methods: (a) imagery, (b) talking with another person about the plan, (c) writing down the plan, or (d) role-playing. After the simulation activity, the student decides if it gave him the confidence and skills to actually use it in a real situation. If not, Roosa recommends additional simulation practice.

Figure 5.5 provides a practice worksheet to facilitate use of the SOCCSS strategy. When using the worksheet, the teacher should do the writing for the student if writing is problematic since the focus is on the strategy, not the task of writing.

SOCCSS
Situation-Options-Consequences-Choices-Strategies-Simulation

Situation

Who was there? _____

_____

What happened? _____

_____

_____

When did it happen? _____

Where did it happen? _____

_____

Why did it happen? _____

_____

_____

Figure 5.5. SOCCSS worksheet.

Options and Consequences

Record options and consequences in the boxes

Option: Rank: _____

Consequence:

Option: Rank: _____

Consequence:

Option: Rank: _____

Consequence:

Option: Rank: _____

Consequence:

Figure 5.5. Continued

Choices

Rank your options and then the chosen best one.
Write it in the box below.

Strategy

Write your new plan of action in the box.

Simulation

Choose one:

1. Find a quiet place to sit and image using your plan.
   Do you think it will work?
2. Talk with someone about your plan. Do you think it's a good plan?
3. Draw a picture or write down what you think might happen when
   you try your plan.
4. Role-play your plan of action to see what happens.

Which one did you choose?

What happened? _____

_____

_____

Figure 5.5. Continued

The *Friends for Me* Social Skills Program

Children with AS have difficulty finding and keeping friends. Frequently unaware of their inappropriate behaviors, reactions, and emotions, and the impact of their inappropriate actions on others, they wonder why they have trouble making friends.

To help them develop friendships, adult intervention that is consistent, systematic, and encouraging is imperative. The school is an excellent place to begin social skills training because it is filled with same-age peers who are available as potential friends. In addition, social workers, psychologists, and speech-language pathologist are available to assist with a social skills training program.

As students begin to understand social language and social rules, their confidence increases and they are ready to begin learning about the concept of friendship. Understanding what friendship is and developing friendships at school will help children function better both in and out school. The *Friends for Me* (Moore, 2002) social skills program is designed to teach friendship skills to children with AS. This motivating program includes 10 activities for teaching social skills in a simple and systematic manner, making it easy for the adult facilitator to use as part of a social skills training program. An outline of the program appears in Table 5.6. The *Friends for Me* program teaches children with AS how to find a friend, be a friend, and keep a friend. Many children with AS want friends and become frustrated when their attempts at finding and keeping friends fail.

Another excellent resource for teaching social skills to children with AS is *Social Skills Training for Students with Asperger Syndrome* (Baker, 2003), which provides step-by-step goals and a format for providing social skills instruction. Children with AS need social skills instruction and guidance in using social skills in the school setting. Therefore, a specific program must be included in their IEP. When writing social interaction goals for students with AS, it is important to include the teachers, paraprofessionals, speech-language pathologist, and parents.

As discussed at the beginning of this chapter, anxiety causes many problems for children with AS, and every attempt should be made to reduce it since learning cannot take place when anxiety levels are high – neither academic nor social learning. Children with AS have great potential; however, they need assistance and direction in overcoming their difficulties due to AS. In the next chapter, emphasis is placed on the importance of committed individuals working together to provide support for children with AS.

TABLE 5.6
Outline of the *Friends for Me* Social Skills Program

Activity 1: *Out of Bounds*
Objective: Learn personal space rules.

Activity 2: *Space Invaders*
Objective: Recognize personal space violations.

Activity 3: *The Name Game*
Objective: Learn names of peers.

Activity 4: *Detective Friend Finder*
Objective: Identify potential friends.

Activity 5: *Begin at the Beginning*
Objective: Begin an interaction.

Activity 6: *Think It, Don't Say It!*
Objective: Refrain from saying offensive comments.

Activity 7: *Professor Problem Solver*
Objective: Identify solutions for a problematic social situation.

Activity 8: *That Sounds Great!*
Objective: Give and receive compliments.

Activity 9: *Say No, Volcano!*
Objective: Recognize anxiety and control emotions.

Activity 10: *Friday Friends*
Objective: Practice social skills in natural settings.

CHAPTER SIX

Team Work

In order for any individualized program to be successful, all persons involved in providing services and support for the student must work as a team. Educational programs for students with AS are no exception. Wherever possible, the team should include the classroom teacher, paraprofessionals, speech-language pathologist, occupational therapist, social worker, psychologist, special education teacher, principal, and the student's parents or guardians. Further-more, the gifted teacher may need to be included for students in the gifted range of ability.

In this chapter we will look at what makes a team work effectively.

Communicating with Staff and Parents

For any team to work effectively, communication is a major component. This is particularly true when dealing with the multiple individuals who must work together to ensure the best possible services for students with AS, including their parents and the students themselves.

Staff

The student with AS needs careful monitoring throughout the day because of her social difficulties, anxiety, and frequent inappropriate responses to unexpected change. If teachers and staff are not familiar with the difficulties students with AS experience, they may perceive their behaviors as defiant, malicious, or indifferent. To prevent this from happening, the entire staff must have an opportunity to learn about the student with AS. This can be accomplished in a number of ways. At the beginning of the school year, the parents or other "expert" on the child's disability can give a presentation to the staff. Or, teachers and therapists can attend workshops or conferences on AS. Information can also be found from numerous websites that offer information, support, and resources for school personnel.

On some days, the student may exhibit no anxiety and deal with change fairly well, but on other days the slightest change in her schedule may send her flying into outer space. When this happens, it is important to notify special teachers and resource staff so they can put extra support in place and be prepared to deal with the student's anxiety or frustration. A simple note to the teacher is all that is needed when a plan for support and intervention is already in place. The note states the problem and identifies the strategy the student needs. When substitute teachers take over your class, be sure to leave a description of the child and her behaviors, as well as the name of a contact person in the school who can provide help should a difficult situation arise (see Table 5.1).

Parents

Ongoing, open home-school communication is also imperative. The following are a few suggestions for how to keep the lines of communication open:

- Use a daily journal in which you and parents notify each other of any concerns or accomplishments.
- Include a section in the assignment notebook where you and parents can add comments.

- Create a change in routine notification system such as a card that goes home to parents the day before a change is to take place (see Change in Routine Card, Figure 3.1).
- Make phone calls to share information. Inform the parents of the time and days that you accept and make calls so they can plan to use an alternate form of communication if they need to relay information at a time or day when you do not receive calls.
- Use e-mail. It is an effective means for communicating as it is flexible and provides a written record.

Students

In addition to communicating with staff members and parents, remember to keep the lines of communication open with the student. Write a quick note to check on him and encourage him to write back to you, or have a Lunch with the Teacher Day (see Figure 6.1) where you invite the student with AS and a couple of his peers to have lunch with you in the classroom. This allows you to check on him in a nonthreatening, informal way. In addition, it is a great way to practice social skills!

---

*You are cordially invited to have
lunch with your teacher on*

_____

*Please join your teacher and her
other guests at your regular lunchtime.
We will be eating lunch in the classroom.*

I look forward to seeing you!

From _____

Figure 6.1. Invitation to have lunch with the teacher.

As you get to know the student, it will be become evident which method of communication works best for the two of you. It is important to keep the lines of communication open to encourage the student to be part of the team because his opinions and perspective should be respected.

Join the Team

When ideas and efforts are collaboratively formed and implemented, the student with AS has the greatest opportunity for achieving academic success and acquiring successful social interaction skills. Everyone on the team should be striving for the same goals for the student:

- Academic achievement equivalent to potential
- Language competence
- Social appropriateness
- Reciprocal interaction
- Flexibility in thinking
- Tolerance for change
- Refinement of special talents

These are just a few of the goals the team may wish to consider when planning for the individual needs of a student with AS. Often parents and teachers ask what the typical goals should be for a student with AS. I encourage them to consider each student's individual needs and talents. Students with AS share similar traits in that their social interaction and communication skills are to some degree impaired, as is their ability to think flexibility. However, I urge all educators and special support staff to treat each child as an *individual* and to keep in mind that students with AS can make progress, both academically and socially. I have seen this with my own son and with other students as well.

Treat each child as an individual and keep in mind that students with AS can make progress.

For years, my husband and I struggled to help our son "fit in," find friends, complete assignments, catch a ball, find his belongings, and stop the TRMs – just to name a few. We could not identify the right parenting book or teaching method to help him. As a baby, my son cried all the time and did not want to be held. When he was a toddler, he was slow to walk and gain his balance and was not interested in feeding himself. During his preschool years, his tantrums and disinterest in other children made it impossible to find friends, both for him and for me. As he entered school, my son's differences became more apparent. One evening, at the beginning of his second-grade school year, his teacher phoned and asked me if I had heard of Asperger Syndrome. She said she knew I was very concerned about my son's differences and asked if the social worker could call me. I told her that I had not heard of Asperger Syndrome, quickly adding that I would be anxiously waiting for the call from the social worker, as my husband and I were desperate to help our son.

That phone call changed our lives forever! My son has reaped the benefits of having an outstanding group of teachers and support staff who devote their hearts to their job, not just their time. They have worked to change my son's world. No longer does he draw pictures of Godzilla all day long at school. No longer does he cover his ears and cry in the lunchroom. No longer does he give up a task before even trying.

Thanks to the efforts of these teachers, my son is achieving up to his potential, is interacting appropriately with his peers, and is able to deal with a change in his schedule! These accomplishments would not have been possible without the support of these caring individuals, who have worked so hard together to help him. The support staff and special education coordinator have all been there, supporting my son's teachers and providing services, as needed.

What My Son Can Do

It used to be that I would tell people what he couldn't do
No running, jumping, catching, throwing
not even tie his shoe

The other boys would ride their bikes and run right past our yard,
my son would watch them as they'd go,
wishing it weren't so hard

Days went by, even months, I can count the years
of sleepless nights filled with pain,
my eyes were filled with tears

No calls, no friends, no confidence, so alone at school
despite our hopes, our prayers, our dreams,
the disability dared to rule

But then my son was given a treasure, this treasure came from you,
and now it is that I tell people
what my son can do

He can kick a ball, play hide & seek and also catch a pass,
perform in the orchestra, take pride in himself,
participate in class

He can laugh and play, sing a solo,
run with children, too
All of this he can do, all because of you!

Like my son, other children with AS can make progress. Teachers, speech-language pathologists, social workers, occupational therapists, inclusion facilitators, and parents working together as a team will make a difference in the lives of children with AS.

The academic interventions and social skills training ideas presented in this book are intended to be used by a team, and they can be adapted and modified to meet a student's unique needs. Children with AS can be helped. It just takes time, thoughtfulness – and a team.

Conclusion

Children with AS can be difficult to teach. To succeed takes patience and understanding, as well as acceptance of their unusual perspective of the world. However, once you begin to understand their mind-set, physical limitations, sensory defensiveness, and need to control, you can begin to gain entrance into their world. As you cross the threshold, grab hold of their hand and slowly bring them out into your world. Autism spectrum disorders are not curable, but their disabling effects can be greatly diminished.

Open the doors to the world for these children,
offer them your hand as they enter,
for the gift you are offering them
will forever enrich their lives.

References

AlphaSmart. www.alphasmart.com

American Psychiatric Association. (1994). *Diagnostic and statistical manual of mental disorders (4th ed.).* Washington, DC: American Psychiatric Association.

Attwood, T. (1998). *Asperger's Syndrome: A guide for parents and professionals.* London: Jessica Kingsley Publishers.

Baker, J. (2003). *Social skills training for students with Asperger Syndrome.* Shawnee Mission, KS: Autism Asperger Publishing Company.

Co:Writer. www.donjohnston.com

Cumine, V., Leach, J., & Stevenson, G. (1998). *Asperger Syndrome: A practical guide for teachers.* London: David Fulton Publishers.

Dragon Naturally Speaking. www.scansoft.com

Dunn, W., Myles, B. S., & Orr, S. (2002). Sensory processing issues associated with Asperger Syndrome: A preliminary investigation. *The Journal of Occupational Therapy, 56*(1), 97-102.

English, E. (1996). *Individualized reading: A complete guide for managing one-on-one instruction.* Cypress, CA: Creative Teaching Press.

Frith, U. (Ed.). (1991). *Autism and Asperger Syndrome.* Cambridge: Cambridge University Press.

Gagnon, E. (2001). *POWER CARDS: Using special interests to motivate children and youth with Asperger Syndrome and autism.* Shawnee Mission, KS: Autism Asperger Publishing Company.

Grandin, T. (1995). *Thinking in pictures: And other reports from my life with autism.* New York: Doubleday.

Gray, C. (1995). *Social stories unlimited: Social stories and comic strip conversations.* Jenison, MI: Jenison Public Schools.

Gray, C., & Gerand, J.D. (1993). Social stories: Improving responses of students with autism with accurate social information. *Focus on Autistic Behavior, 8,* 1-10.

Handwriting Without Tears. www.hwtears.com

Koegel, R., & Koegel, L. (1995). *Teaching children with autism.* Baltimore, MD: Paul H. Brookes Publishing.

Lifter, K. (2000). *Developmental Play Assessment (DPA) Instrument.* In K. Gitlin-Weiner, A. Sandgrund, & C. E. Schaefer (Eds.), *Play diagnosis and assessment.* New York: John Wiley & Sons.

McClannahan, L., & Krantz, P. (1999). *Activity schedules for children with autism: Teaching independent behavior.* Bethesda, MD: Woodbine House.

McGuinness, R. (2000). *Cloze encounters.* New York: World Teachers Press.

Michael Thompson Productions & Bligh, S. (2000). *Social language groups.* Naperville, IL: Author.

Moore, G. (1998). *Cloze in on language.* New York: World Teachers Press.

Moore, S.T. (2002). *Friends for me: A social skills program for children with Asperger Syndrome.* Shawnee Mission, KS: Autism Asperger Publishing Company.

Myles, B.S., & Adreon, D. (2001). *Asperger Syndrome and adolescence: Practical solutions for school success.* Shawnee Mission, KS: Autism Asperger Publishing Company.

Myles, B.S., Cook, K.T., Miller, N.E., Rinner, L., & Robbins, L.A. (2000). *Asperger Syndrome and sensory issues: Practical solutions for making sense of the world.* Shawnee Mission, KS: Autism Asperger Publishing Company.

Myles, B.S., & Simpson, R.L. (1998). *Asperger Syndrome: A guide for educators and parents.* Austin, TX: Pro-Ed.

Myles, B.S., & Southwick, J. (1999). *Asperger Syndrome and difficult moments: Practical solutions for tantrums, rage, and meltdowns.* Shawnee Mission, KS: Autism Asperger Publishing Company.

Nowicki, S., & Duke, M. (1992). *Helping the child who doesn't fit in.* Atlanta, GA: Peachtree Publishers.

Quill, K. A. (1995). *Teaching children with autism: Strategies to enhance communication and socialization.* London: International Thomas Publishing Company.

Quill, K. A. (2000). *DO-WATCH-LISTEN-SAY: Social communication intervention for children with autism.* Baltimore, MD: Paul H. Brookes.

Savner, J., & Myles, B.S. (2000). *Making visual supports work in the home and community: Strategies for individuals with autism and Asperger Syndrome.* Shawnee Mission, KS: Autism Asperger Publishing Company.

Sundbye, R., & McCoy, L.J. (2001). *Helping the struggling reader: What to teach and how to teach it (2nd ed.).* Lawrence, KS: Curriculum Solutions.

Swaggart, B., Gagnon, E., Bock, S., Earles, T., Quinn, C., Myles, B.S., & Simpson, R. (1995). Using social stories to teach social and behavioral skills to children with autism. *Focus on Autistic Behavior, 10,* 1-16.

Wilde, L.D., Koegel, L.K. & Koegel, R.L. (1992). *Increasing success in school through priming: A training manual.* Santa Barbara: University of California.

Willey, L.H. (1999). *Pretending to be normal: Living with Asperger's Syndrome.* London: Jessica Kingsley Publishers.

Willey, L.H. (2001). *Asperger Syndrome in the family: Redefining normal.* London: Jessica Kingsley Publishers.

Winner, E. (1996). *Gifted children: Myths and realities.* New York: Basic Books.

Wolfberg, P.J. (1999). *Play and imagination in children with autism.* New York: Teachers College Press.

Wolfberg, P.J. (2002). *Peer play and the autism spectrum: The art of guiding children's socialization and imagination.* Shawnee Mission, KS: Autism Asperger Publishing Company.

Write:OutLoud. www.donjohnston.com

Index